The New Field Guide to the U.S. Economy

The New Field Guide to the U. S. Economy

A Compact and Irreverent Guide to Economic Life in America

Nancy Folbre and The Center for Popular Economics

Designed by Robert Dworak

The New Press, New York

Grateful acknowledgment is made to the following for permission to reprint previously published material: Kirk Anderson, Jeff Danziger and the Los Angeles Times Syndicate, Norman Dog, Robert Englehardt, Mike Konopacki, Peter Hannan, Nicole Hollander, Gary Huck, Howard Saunders, Mike Thompson and Copley News Service, Tom Toles and the Universal Press Syndicate, Dan Wassermann and the Los Angeles Times Syndicate, Matt Wuerker.

ISBN 1-56584-153-0
Library of Congress Catalog Card Number 95-67537

Published in the United States by The New Press, New York
Distributed by W. W. Norton & Company, Inc., New York

Established in 1990 as a major alternative to the large, commercial publishing houses, The New Press is the first full-scale nonprofit American book publisher outside of the university presses. The Press is operated editorially in the public interest, rather than for private gain; it is committed to publishing in innovative ways works of educational, cultural and community value that, despite their intellectual merits, might not normally be commercially viable. The New Press's editorial offices are located at the City University of New York.

Book design by Robert Dworak
Production management by Kim Waymer
Printed in the United States of America

95 96 97 98   9 8 7 6 5 4 3 2 1

Contents

Chapter 7: Health

Chapter 8: Environment

Chapter 9: Macroeconomics

Chapter 10: The Global Economy

Toolkit

Sources

Glossary

Acknowledgments

The New Field Guide was motivated by the ongoing teaching needs of the Center for Popular Economics (CPE). Many members of the collective contributed in one way or another, digging up numbers or commenting on drafts or suggesting cartoons.

Some individuals made major contributions. Pierre Laliberte served as primary research assistant and played an important role in defining both the content and the illustration of the book. Elissa Braunstein helped conceptualize and research the chapter on energy and the environment. Jim Westrich provided the basic material for the chapter on health. James Heintz took charge of the fine-tuning that involved checking sources and doing final updates.

Without Susan Stinson's general enthusiasm and successful fund-raising, the project would never have been undertaken. As Director of the Center, Lisa Nelson helped keep both it and this project on an even keel. For their suggestions regarding individual chapters, special thanks to CPE members Randy Albelda, Sam Bowles, Jim Crotty, Jerry Epstein, Ellen Frank, Tony Guglielmi, Dave Kristjanson, Tom Riddell, Judy Robinson, and Val Voorheis.

Many individuals outside the Center also made enormous contributions. In addition to serving as designer and desktop publisher, Robert Dworak managed the entire data collection process. Glen Ruga of Visual Communications served as a consultant to the design process. Marc Breslow, Bryan Snyder, and other members of the Dollars and Sense collective offered constructive comments and criticisms. Barry Bergman of the National Priorities Project, Randy Kehler of the Working Group on Electoral Democracy, and Edie Rasell of the Economic Policy Institute provided important ideas and numbers. Ann Sandhorst advised us on permissions. Yu Quing Shen provided research assistance.

This project was inspired by the work of rare and wonderful artists who know how to make economists smile. Nicholas Blechman (aka Knickerbocker) and Russell Christian illustrated many pages with wit and wisdom. Special thanks to those cartoonists who donated all or a substantial portion of their permission fees: Nicole Hollander, Gary Huck, Mike Konopacki, Tom Tomorrow, Dan Wassermann, and Matt Wuerker.

André Schiffrin and Ellen Reeves of the New Press gave us excellent guidance from start to finish.

Thanks are due the progressive foundations and individual donors who provided vital support for this book:

Marjorie Abel
John Mayer
Robin Lloyd
The Funding Exchange
RESIST Fund
Samuel Rubin Foundation
The Unitarian Universalist Veatch Program.

We are also grateful to those who have helped keep the Center for Popular Economics going through thick and thin. The following have made significant donations over the last five years:

Anonymous
Bonnie Anderson
Harriet Barlow and the Blue Mountain Center
The Boston Women's Fund
Samuel Bowles
Bread & Roses Community Fund
Collective Copies
James Crotty
Ann Dickinson
Kevin Eastman
Jean Entine
W. H. and Carol Bernstein Ferry
Ben Fiscella
John Fitzgerald
The Funding Exchange
John Kenneth and Kitty Galbraith
Herbert Gintis
Connie Hall
Richard and Carole Harmon
Haymarket People's Fund
Jonathan Hiatt
Ann Jones
Marc Kitchel
Charlotte Klose
John Lapham
The Limantour Fund
Dr. Bernard and Louise Lown
John D. and Catherine T. MacArthur Foundation
Stephen and Frederique Marglin
Sunanda Markus
Dale Melcher and William Newman
Valerie Miller
Open Meadows Foundation
Pennsylvania Humanities Council
Christina Platt
Warren Plaut Memorial Fund
Presbyterian Women's Thank Offering
RESIST Fund
Tom Riddell
Samuel Rubin Foundation
John Simmons
The Unitarian Universalist Veatch Program
United Church Board for Homeland Ministries
Woods Charitable Fund
Robert Paul and Susan Wolff.

The Center for Popular Economics offers economic literacy programs for activists and organizers. For more information on workshops and summer programs, contact us: P. O. Box 785, Amherst, MA 01004. (413-545-0743)

Chapter 1 **Owners**

Russell Christian

Who owns what in the United States? This chapter looks at the distribution of family wealth and the structure of corporate power. It also considers some ways the ownership of wealth might be changed.

Them that's got shall get. Individuals compete against each other in the capitalist marketplace, but their success is partly determined by what they bring with them to the market. Some people bring nothing but their desire to work. Others bring expensive skills or considerable wealth; when they leave, they usually take home even more.

Chart 1.1 shows that the richest 20% of all families own 45% of all wealth. But there are even bigger differences in wealth within this high-income group. And these differences are getting bigger. As *Chart 1.2* points out, the richest 1% of all families increased their piece of the wealth pie in the 1980s.

Most families with low and middle incomes use their earnings to buy things like a house or a car. But the very wealthy enjoy substantial income from the ownership of assets like stocks, bonds, and investment properties. As *Chart 1.3* shows, this group is a small minority. Most people rely on earnings rather than property income. *Chart 1.4* helps explain why. Stocks and bonds are concentrated in relatively few hands.

The richest people in the U.S., however, are not the richest in the world. *Chart 1.5* puts five leading billionaire families in global perspective and highlights the important role of inheritance. Next, *Chart 1.6* focuses on an important subset of the rich, America's corporate executives, who typically enjoy lucrative stock options. In 1993, they earned more in two days than the average factory worker earns in a year.

Wealth can buy more than a high standard of living. Sometimes political influence and economic power come up for sale. *Chart 1.7* details the relative size of contributions that business, labor, and single-issue organizations make to political action committees, while *Chart 1.8* examines the important role of virtually unregulated "soft money" donated to political parties rather than to specific campaigns.

Corporations exercise far more economic power than individuals or families. When they compete fiercely with one another, their influence is limited. But as the next four charts show, competition isn't always the rule. *Chart 1.9* points out that many major industries are dominated by large firms. *Chart 1.10* traces slow but steady increases in the share of all assets owned by the top 100 industrial firms. *Chart 1.11* does the same for the banking industry. *Chart 1.12* illustrates the economic size of the three largest companies in the world, which is far greater than that of many small countries.

But perhaps these institutions are less monolithic than they seem. The employee stock-ownership plans described in *Chart 1.13* haven't given workers much control over corporate wealth, but might, in the future. And while few workers enjoy any control over their pension funds, the figures in *Chart 1.14* suggest how powerful that kind of control could be.

1.1 Wealth and Income in the U.S.

"The rich are different from you and me," said F. Scott Fitzgerald. "Yes," said Ernest Hemingway. "They have more money." More specifically, they have more wealth, an accumulation of money and other assets that can generate income.

The technical term most often used to describe wealth ownership is "net worth," the value of wealth (in the form of savings, investments, and property) minus debt.

The Census Bureau gives a broad picture of the relationship between wealth and income, though it warns that high-income households significantly underreport their assets.

In 1991, the top 20% of households, with incomes of more than $53,448, owned 45% of all household wealth. The bottom 20%, with incomes of less than $12,852, owned about 7%.

Distribution of household wealth, by income quintiles, 1991
(upper limits of income categories in parentheses)

Income group	Median net worth	Share of total net worth
Top 20% (no upper limit)	$123,166	45%
Next 20% (up to $53,448)	$49,204	20%
Next 20% (up to $34,968)	$28,859	16%
Next 20% (up to $22,944)	$19,191	12%
Bottom 20% (up to $12,852)	$5,224	7%

1.2 Very Rich, Getting Richer

"The 1980s: A Very Good Time for the Rich"—that's the way the *New York Times* described the results of a recent study released by the Congressional Budget Office. The study, focusing on the wealthy, shows that the top 1% increased their share of net worth, or wealth, from 31% to 37% between 1983 and 1989. Their share now exceeds that owned by the bottom 90% of all families. Much of this wealth will be passed on, untouched, to the next generation. The top tax rate on income fell from 90% during the Kennedy years to 31% during the Reagan years.

Another study shows that the crème de la crème reaped most of the gains from the booming 1980s. They enjoyed 60% of all after-tax income gains between 1977 and 1989. Over the same period, the poor got poorer: The income of the bottom 20% of American families fell by 10%.

Share of net worth of U.S. families

	1983	1989
Richest 1%	31%	37%
Next richest 9%	35%	31%
Remaining 90%	33%	32%

1.3 Who Gets Money from What?

Why does the nightly news say more about stock prices than about real wages? Most people get most of their income from work, not from property, and the state of the labor market affects their lives far more directly than the stock market.

In 1992, 74% of all persons 15 and over took home some kind of paycheck; a small group of 7% enjoyed self-employment income.

Most others were retirees relying on Social Security, which remains a far more important source of income to most elderly than private pensions.

Because they had some money in savings accounts, about 58% of all adults earned some interest in 1992. The average amount, however, was little more than $1,000. Fewer people received income from dividends or from rents, royalties, estates, or trusts (14% and 7%, respectively). And because many of these people received very small amounts, the average income from these sources was very low.

Knickerbocker

Sources of personal income in 1992
(persons 15 and over)

Source	% with income from source	Mean income
Earnings	74%	$22,667
Nonfarm self-employment	7%	$16,523
Social Security	20%	$6,412
Pensions	8%	$9,454
Interest	58%	$1,266
Dividends	14%	$1,758
Rents, royalties, estates, or trusts	7%	$3,421

1.4 What Do the Wealthy Own?

More families in this country own stock than belong to labor unions (22% compared with 16%). But few own very much. Most stocks, bonds, and other financial assets are owned by the richest 10% of the population.

Most middle-class wealth is concentrated in homes and cars, though many families enjoy pension plans and other savings for old age. In recent years, middle-class investment in the stock market, particularly in mutual funds, has increased.

People who enjoy considerable amounts of investment income generally like high interest rates, which offer them a higher rate of return on savings. While they benefit from stock market and real estate booms, they shiver at the thought of inflation, which often erodes the value of investment income.

Share of total value of family-owned assets in 1989

The richest 1% of families held:

45% of all nonresidential real estate
62% of all business assets
49% of all publicly held stock
78% of all bonds

The richest 10% of families held:

80% of all nonresidential real estate
91% of all business assets
85% of all stocks
94% of all bonds

1.5 The Richest People in the World

Picture the Sultan of Brunei eating a Mars Bar at a WalMart store built by a Japanese developer who advertises with Advance Publications. The 5 largest fortunes in the world would all be represented in one room, with a gilt sign indicating that they collectively represent almost $100 billion in assets.

Where did all that wealth come from? *Fortune* publishes photographs and brief descriptions of world billionaires but doesn't describe their history. *Forbes* runs an annual feature on the richest families in the U.S. that provides more details. Some founders started from scratch, like Sam Moore Walton, who gradually built a highly successful chain of retail stores. But more than half of the richest 400 people in this country largely inherited their wealth, just like the Sultan of Brunei.

The top 5 fortunes in the world, 1993

Name	Billions of $US	Source of wealth
Sultan of Brunei	$37	Investments, global real estate, oil and gas
The Walton family	$23.5	38% of WalMart Stores
The Mars family	$14.0	100% of Mars, Inc., M&M/Mars, Uncle Ben's Rice, others
Minoru Mori Akira Mori	$13.0	Building and development, real estate
Samuel I. Newhouse, Jr. Donald Newhouse	$10.0	100% of Advance Publications

1.6 CEO Pay

America's best-paid workers are also owners. Most of the income of chief executive officers (CEOs) of big corporations comes from options to purchase company stock under favorable terms. In 1993, Michael Eisner, chairman of Walt Disney Company, earned $750,000 in salary but $202 million in long-term compensation. The total amount almost equals the gross national product of Grenada.

The relative, as well as the absolute, level of CEO compensation has increased dramatically over time. In 1993, they took home 149 times as much as an average factory worker. Back in 1960, they earned only about 40 times as much. In Japan, in 1992, CEOs earned only 32 times as much as workers.

Do companies get what they pay for? Every year, *Business Week* asks this question and usually concludes that there is no discernible relationship between pay and performance. Informal, backslapping collusion between CEOs, boards of directors, and consulting firms encourages rapid salary increases. The Securities and Exchange Commission recently created new regulations requiring firms to disclose executive pay packages to their stockholders.

Average factory worker's pay compared with average CEO's pay, 1993

◀── Factory worker: $25,317

Chief Executive Officer: $3,772,000

1.7 The Price of Influence

Money talks, and its electoral voice is deafening. Many different individuals, companies, and political action committees (PACs) gave money to congressional campaigns in 1991-92. But business outspent other groups by a wide margin, investing more than $295 million in its favorite candidates.

Organized labor raised little more than 15% of that amount (a total of $43 million). Individual unions, unlike individual firms, did not donate, and labor contributions to PACS were relatively low. Other groups, including single-issue types such as environmentalist organizations, exercised even less financial influence.

The system of private financing for public elections makes it difficult for candidates to win an election without backing from wealthy individuals and groups. It also leaves elected officials beholden to those who helped finance their campaign.

Total PAC and individual contributions in congressional campaigns, 1991-92
(millions of $)

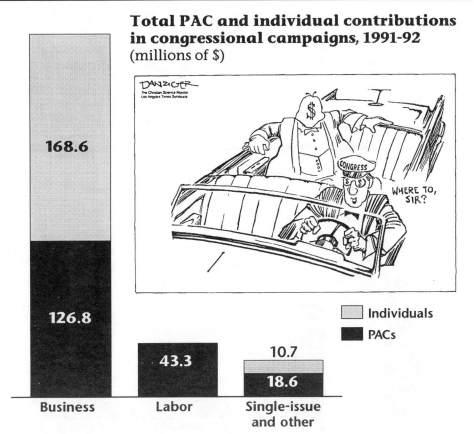

Individuals

PACs

168.6		
126.8	43.3	10.7
		18.6
Business	Labor	Single-issue and other

1.8 Soft Money, Hard Power

If you have a lot of money and want to buy some power, political action committees are inconvenient: Federal law limits the size of individual contributions to PACs. That's why many big shots prefer to make "soft money" donations to political parties. In theory, such donations are intended to support party building, rather than specific candidates; in practice, the distinction is meaningless.

In the 1992 election, "soft money" totaled more than $88 million. Most of this money, 60%, came from those who contributed more than $50,000. Half of the total came from just 265 donors. There's nothing soft about that kind of influence.

The very rich, of course, don't need to ask for donations. They can spend unlimited amounts of their own money on their own campaigns for office: The Supreme Court has ruled that any restrictions would infringe on their rights to free speech. Of course, this kind of free speech is too expensive for most.

Concentration of soft money in 1992

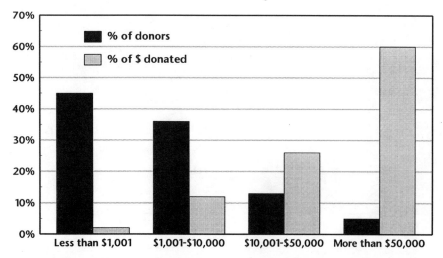

- % of donors
- % of $ donated

Less than $1,001 | $1,001-$10,000 | $10,001-$50,000 | More than $50,000

IF THE POOR DON'T LIKE IT, LET 'EM BUY THEIR *OWN* SENATORS!

Tom Tomorrow

1.9 Market Dominance

How many brands of breakfast cereal can you name? There are more than a hundred. But if you look closer, they are all pretty much the same. And so are their producers: Three large firms (Kellogg, General Mills, and General Foods) control nearly 90% of sales.

Pure monopolies are rare, but many leading industries are dominated by just one, two, or three firms. Even if they compete fiercely in some respects (such as inventing new cereal names), they have a lot to gain by collaboration.

Aircraft purchasers depend heavily on Boeing and McDonnell-Douglas, the two firms that account for about 80% of all sales in the United States. Photographers usually buy Kodak film, which has accounted for over 75% of all film sales for almost 100 years. And long-distance phone calls go A.T.&T. most of the time.

Market dominance means higher prices and fewer choices for consumers, and higher profits for owners.

Nicole Hollander

Percentage of industries controlled by large firms in 1993

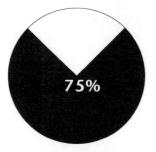

75%

Photographic film

80%

Aircraft

90%

Cereals

65%

Long-distance telephone

1.10 Economic Concentration

As names like United Brands imply, many U.S. firms are engaged in more than one line of business: They are conglomerates. They may not dominate any one industry, but a look at their share of total corporate assets reveals a great concentration of economic power.

By this measure, the top 100 industrial corporations in the U.S. have substantially increased in relative size. In 1993, their combined assets amounted to 30% of total assets of nonfinancial corporations, compared with 22% in 1961.

On the other hand, foreign competition has diminished the economic power of many large U.S. firms. The trend might look different if we looked at the share of the top 100 as a share of the assets of all multinational corporations, including those based in other countries.

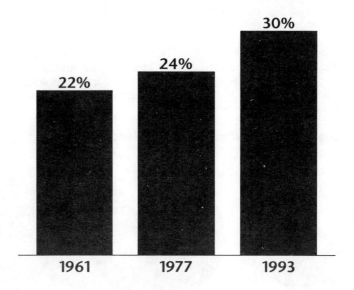

Assets of Fortune top 100 industrial corporations as a percent of assets of all nonfinancial corporations

- 1961: 22%
- 1977: 24%
- 1993: 30%

1.11 Bank Behemoths

Knickerbocker

If your local bank hasn't yet been swallowed up by a bigger one, it's behind the times. With the deregulation of banking, mergers and closings have led to consolidation. The number of U.S. bank holding companies shrank from 13,000 to 10,000 between 1981 and 1991.

The result? Increases in the level of bank concentration. The largest 50 banks accounted for 52% of all domestic banking assets in 1989, compared with 41% in 1970. If current trends continue, they will control at least 63% by the year 2010.

Competition among banks will inevitably slacken. Many banks will find it easier to raise fees, charge higher interest rates on loans, and offer lower interest rates on savings. As *Fortune* notes, prospects are bright for those who own stock in banks, but "Don't expect borrowers and depositors to celebrate."

Share of domestic banking assets owned by largest 5% of banking organizations

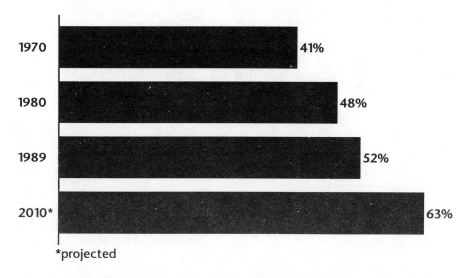

Year	Share
1970	41%
1980	48%
1989	52%
2010*	63%

*projected

1.12 The Size of Multinational Enterprise

In its dealings with many small countries around the globe, the U.S. puts a big emphasis on democracy and human rights. Yet, these concepts are seldom applied to large multinational corporations, economic entities that are often larger than nations. The worldwide sales of Ford, Exxon, and General Motors in 1992 were far greater than the value of all goods sold (gross domestic product) in countries like Honduras, Zimbabwe, or the Philippines.

The sheer size of multinational enterprises makes them difficult to oversee or regulate. Their ability to move in and out of countries gives them considerable bargaining power in their dealings with local employees and host countries. If labor laws or environmental regulations in one country become too onerous, they can simply move to another.

Worldwide sales of the three largest companies in the world in 1992 and gross domestic product of some developing countries in 1992
(in billions of $US)

Russell Christian

Honduras	Zimbabwe	Philippines	Ford Motor	Exxon	GMC
2.4	5.3	43.9	98.3	105.9	126

1.13 ESOP's Fable?

Worker ownership is one alternative to the current concentration of wealth in the U.S. economy. Many people can buy shares in the companies they work for through employee stock-ownership plans (ESOPs). In the 1980s, changes in tax laws made the plans very popular, but hard times in the 1990s put a damper on their expansion. In 1993, about 11 million people, more than 8% of all employees, belonged to some form of ESOP.

The notion that stock ownership automatically gives workers control over their jobs is an ESOP's fable. The stock shares are commonly held in trust for the employees by a bank or other institution, so most workers share the risk of ownership without enjoying any real control.

Still, some ESOPs encourage worker participation and challenge conventional corporate culture.

Percent of employees enrolled in employee stock-ownership plans

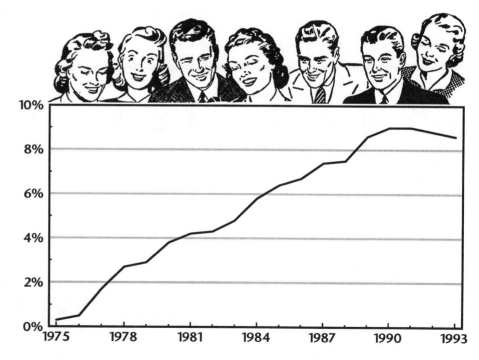

1.14 Pension Fund Capital

If workers gained some control over how their pension funds are invested, they could change the face of corporate America. In 1991, the total assets of corporate, state, and local employee benefit funds amounted to over $3 trillion. According to one recent estimate, about 40% of all corporate stocks and 50% of bonds were held by private and public pension funds.

Currently, funds are strictly prohibited from using any but "prudent financial" criteria in investing, which means that workers may find themselves providing capital for firms that are busting unions or harming the environment. Also, most pension fund capital (70%) is in the hands of employers who invest it as they see fit. During the 1980s, many corporations tapped into pension funds as a cheap source of financing. As a result, about half of all single-employer plans are suspected to be in trouble.

Pension fund assets
(trillions of $1992)

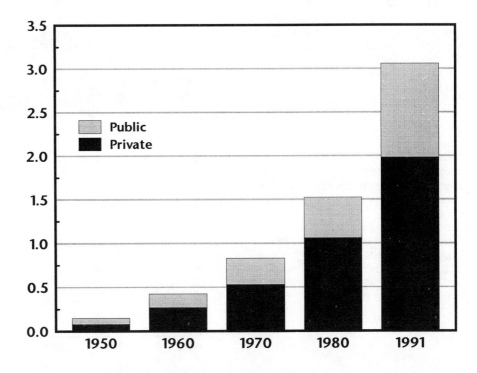

Chapter 2 **Workers**

Russell Christian

What kinds of work do people do? How much do they get paid? How many people are unemployed, and why? This chapter traces the answers to these four questions and shows how they are interrelated.

After many years of rapid growth, the size of the labor force may be leveling off. *Chart 2.1* shows that women's participation in wage employment is not increasing as fast as it once was, while men's participation continues to decline. Part of the explanation lies in increases in the number of workers who have given up looking for a job.

The types of jobs available are very different to-day from what they were in 1950. The service sector was important back then; but as *Chart 2.2* illustrates, it now accounts for over 70% of all employment. One reason this has a huge impact on the labor force is that average wages in services are far below average wages in manufacturing (see *Chart 2.3*). Also, many service industries have a high demand for part-time and temporary workers. Some people prefer that type of work, but there has been an enormous increase in the number of people who simply can't find a full-time or permanent job (*Chart 2.4*).

Once upon a time, earnings increased substantially every year. *Chart 2.5* tracks the steady growth of hourly earnings, corrected for inflation, between 1950 and 1972. After that year, wages dipped, recovered, and started sagging. By 1993, they had fallen to about the same level as in 1968. A look at trends in weekly earnings by race in *Chart 2.6* shows that while all groups experienced a decline, African-Americans and Latinos were hurt the most.

Workers at the bottom of the pay scale have suffered the most, partly because increases in the federal minimum wage, documented in *Chart 2.7*, have not been sufficient to compensate for inflation. Of course, pay is not the only component of worker compensation. In the 1970s and 1980s, employer contributions to pension plans and health insurance helped make up for declining wages, especially among better-paid workers. But as *Chart 2.8* indicates, the era of generous benefits is over, and cutbacks are the order of the day.

All these trends have contributed to a noticeable increase in inequality among workers. Measured relative to the poverty level for a family of 4 in *Chart 2.9*, the percentage of workers earning what can only be termed subsistence wages increased substantially between 1973 and 1991. Young people have been particularly hard hit. *Chart 2.10* shows that entry-level wages have declined, even for college graduates.

Unemployment rates are painfully high, and young people, African-Americans, and Latinos are most affected. Official figures understate the actual extent of joblessness. *Chart 2.11* displays the variation in rates across groups in 1993, while *Chart 2.12* traces the upward trend over time. The fastest-growing group of unemployed are job losers affected by widespread layoffs and restructuring. *Chart 2.13* presents some salient facts about displaced workers. *Chart 2.14* places U.S. unemployment rates in international perspective, pointing out that Germany and Japan are utilizing their workforces more efficiently.

Historically, trade unions have served as a powerful tool for increasing the living standards of their members and, to some extent, those of workers in general. But as *Chart 2.15* demonstrates, union membership has been falling for a long time and has only recently begun to level off. Unions are now beginning to adapt to industrial restructuring and renew their organizing efforts. *Chart 2.16* emphasizes the important role that women, people of color, and government employees now play in the union movement.

2.1 Slower Growth in the Labor Force

Knickerbocker

Women doing more paid work, men doing less: That was the trend from 1950 until recently. Now women's entrance into the paid labor force is leveling off.

Maybe people are just running out of time. Further increases in hours devoted to paid employment would mean even fewer hours for running errands and caring for family members. If women could persuade men to take on more responsibilities for these tasks, male and female labor force participation rates might eventually converge.

Declines in male labor force participation rates since 1950 don't reflect any increase in the number of househusbands. Rather, expanding Social Security benefits have led to earlier retirement for many. In addition, large numbers of poorly educated men, discouraged by persistently high levels of unemployment, have stopped looking for work.

U.S. labor force participation rates, 1950-94

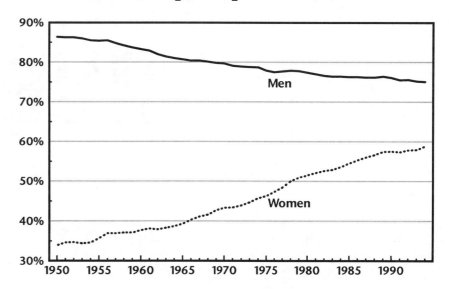

2.2 Services Versus Products

Most workers today provide services rather than produce things. As early as 1950, more than 50% were employed in service jobs, a catchall for diverse economic activities that usually involve transactions with people or information.

Since then, the percentage has increased to more than 75%, initially as a result of declines in agriculture and related activities. The share of employees in manufacturing, mining, and construction declined steeply after 1970; by 1990, it accounted for only about 22% of the total.

More manufactured goods are being imported from other countries, so there is less demand for labor to produce them here.

The changing composition of employment

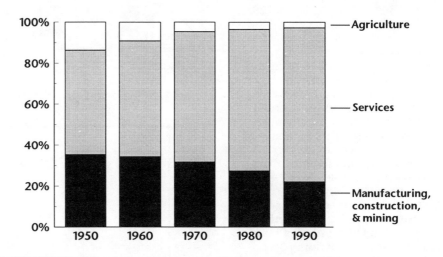

WE CAN GIVE YOU A JOB, BUT NOT LIKE THE INDUSTRIAL JOB YOU LOST

IT OFFERS LOWER PAY, FEWER BENEFITS AND LESS SECURITY

IS THIS WHAT THEY MEAN BY THE "SERVICE ECONOMY"?

THAT'S RIGHT — YOU'LL BE DOING US A BIG SERVICE

2.3 Good-bye Factory Jobs

Nearly 24 million jobs were created between 1979 and 1993. All of this growth took place in the service sector of the economy. In fact, the goods-producing sector (manufacturing, mining, and construction) lost 3.2 million jobs over that period, a decline of 12%; the service sector gained almost 24 million, an increase of 38%.

This shift has had a depressing effect on average wages. Factory work has never been fun. But traditionally it offered secure and relatively well-paying jobs to men and women who were willing to work hard, whatever their educational attainments. Not anymore. Many factory workers have lost their jobs due to plant closings and have been unable to find new ones.

The boom in services evokes images of well-paid lawyers, business consultants, and financial experts. But while some service jobs offer high pay, most involve fairly unskilled work like pushing brooms, waiting on customers, and entering data into computers. These jobs don't provide much take-home pay and often don't provide much in benefits.

The average hourly compensation (earnings plus benefits) in all services in 1993 was $15.51, compared with $20.22 in goods production.

Change in employment, by sector, 1979-93

38%

Service-producing

-12%

Goods-producing

Russell Christian

2.4 Hello Temps

Maybe you'll come back tomorrow, and maybe you won't. That's what the fastest-growing category of employment is all about. Temporary jobs expanded by 211% between 1970 and 1990, compared with 54% for all employment. Manpower Inc. is now the country's largest employer.

Some people don't want to work full-time. Voluntary part-time work increased slightly faster than all employment, but involuntary part-time jobs (in which workers really wanted full-time work) grew much faster.

Most temporary and part-time jobs are in clerical and retail services. Employers like such arrangements not only because they are flexible but also because they can avoid paying benefits like health insurance.

Change in types of employment, 1970-90

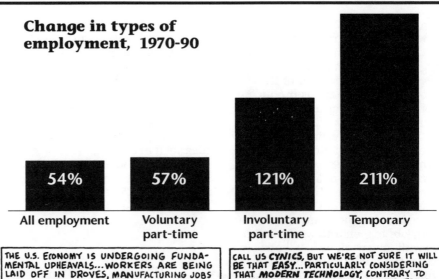

All employment	Voluntary part-time	Involuntary part-time	Temporary
54%	57%	121%	211%

THE U.S. ECONOMY IS UNDERGOING FUNDAMENTAL UPHEAVALS... WORKERS ARE BEING LAID OFF IN DROVES, MANUFACTURING JOBS ARE DISAPPEARING OVERSEAS, AND THE SINGLE LARGEST EMPLOYER IN THIS COUNTRY IS A *TEMP AGENCY*... BUT DON'T WORRY—THE *EXPERTS* HAVE A *SOLUTION*...

YES—WE'LL SIMPLY *RETRAIN* EVERYONE!

...IN SOME VAGUE AND UNSPECIFIED MANNER...

CALL US *CYNICS*, BUT WE'RE NOT SURE IT WILL BE THAT *EASY*... PARTICULARLY CONSIDERING THAT *MODERN TECHNOLOGY*, CONTRARY TO POPULAR BELIEF, MAY ACTUALLY BE *ELIMINATING* MORE JOBS THAN IT IS *CREATING*— AS EXEMPLIFIED BY THE 47,000 *POSTAL WORKERS* ABOUT TO BE REPLACED BY COMPUTERS...

MAYBE WE CAN RETRAIN THEM TO BE *ECONOMISTS*...

ULP!

Tom Tomorrow

2.5 Declining Hourly Wages

Many workers have the glum feeling that it's getting harder and harder to make a decent living, and they are right. From 1950 to the mid-1970s, real average hourly earnings steadily increased, giving most ordinary people a sense of economic progress. After 1973, that progress ground to a halt.

Inflation was the initial cause; wages simply didn't keep up with sudden price increases in 1974 and 1979. But even when inflation abated in the 1980s, real wages remained stagnant. In 1994, the average hourly wage, at $10.46, was lower than it had been in 1968, at $10.61 (in constant $1992, accounting for inflation).

Some workers, especially those belonging to unions, enjoyed increases in the value of benefits such as health insurance that helped compensate for smaller paychecks. But in recent years, these too have declined.

Average hourly earnings, 1950-94
(private nonagricultural nonsupervisory or production workers, in $1992)

2.6 Weekly Paychecks

No matter how you look at it, workers are making do with less. Earnings can be measured in many different ways. Data on median weekly earnings are collected for all full-time workers (rather than just production workers). As a result of low hourly earnings, people now work slightly more hours per week than they used to.

The picture here resembles trends in average hourly earnings. Despite recent increases, median weekly earnings are still lower than they were in 1973. Also, racial and ethnic differences in earnings have become more extreme.

The Census Bureau did not publish distinct statistics on African-Americans and Latinos until 1979, making it difficult to evaluate long-run trends. But people of color in general narrowed the pay gap with whites substantially between 1970 and 1978. After 1979, that gap increased.

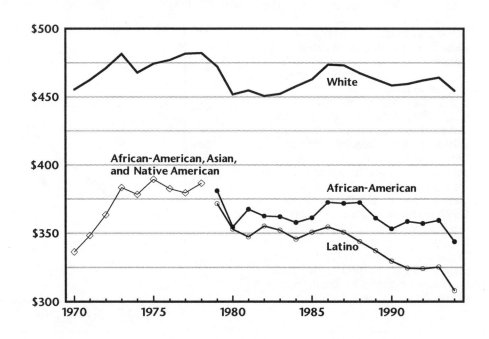

Median weekly earnings of full-time workers, 1970-94 ($1992)

2.7 The Minimal Minimum Wage

Life is harsh in low-wage America. Minimum wages are supposed to set a standard of decency, but that standard has fallen: The real value of the minimum wage in 1994 was lower than it was in 1950.

In the 1950s and 1960s, Congress boosted the minimum wage several times, more than enough to compensate for inflation. In 1968 it reached a peak, and since then it has trended downward.

The low minimum wage means poverty for many families. At $4.25 an hour in 1994, a full-time worker brought home less than $9,000 a year, far below the poverty level established by the Census Bureau for a family of four.

Some economists insist that a higher minimum wage would discourage employers from hiring. Others argue that an increase would improve standards of living and increase consumer demand, prompting employers to hire more workers.

Real minimum wage, 1950-94 ($1992)

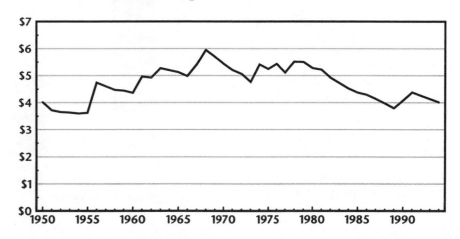

2.8 Good-bye Benefits

People depend on more than the pay in their paycheck. In the 1960s, employers began providing many workers with relatively generous benefit packages, taking advantage of the fact that these were not subject to taxation. As these benefits became more and more expensive, however, employers began to change their minds.

The decline in health insurance benefits has been particularly striking. In 1980, employers paid all premiums for 71% of all full-time employees in medium and large firms. By 1993, only 37% of employees were fully covered. The number with any coverage at all also declined substantially.

Many retirement benefits have been downgraded from plans that guarantee a certain benefit to those that simply make a defined contribution to a retirement account.

Part-time and temporary workers, as well as those who work for small firms, are even less likely to enjoy health and retirement benefits.

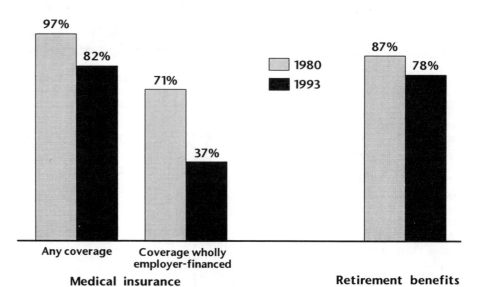

Percent of full-time employees enrolled in employee benefit programs
(medium and large firms)

- 1980
- 1993

Medical insurance
- Any coverage: 97% (1980), 82% (1993)
- Coverage wholly employer-financed: 71% (1980), 37% (1993)

Retirement benefits: 87% (1980), 78% (1993)

2.9 Greater Earnings Inequality

More and more workers are stuck in jobs that don't pay them enough to support a family above the poverty line. In 1973, 24% of all workers fit that category. By 1993, 27% of all workers earned an hourly wage too low to adequately support a family of 4.

Differences among wage earners have increased. Highly educated professionals and managers now enjoy a huge wage premium over less skilled workers who once enjoyed relatively well-paying manufacturing jobs. Similar trends are apparent in Europe but are not as extreme as in the United States because they have been buffered by strong unions and more sympathetic state policies (such as higher minimum wages).

Workers of color in this country have been disproportionately affected. In 1993, 36% of African-Americans and 43% of Latinos earned hourly wages that were below the poverty level for a family of 4.

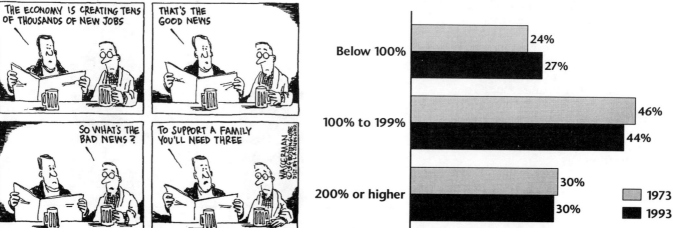

THE ECONOMY IS CREATING TENS OF THOUSANDS OF NEW JOBS

THAT'S THE GOOD NEWS

SO WHAT'S THE BAD NEWS?

TO SUPPORT A FAMILY YOU'LL NEED THREE

Workers' wages relative to the poverty level for a family of 4

Below 100%
- 24% (1973)
- 27% (1993)

100% to 199%
- 46% (1973)
- 44% (1993)

200% or higher
- 30% (1973)
- 30% (1993)

☐ 1973
■ 1993

2.10 Young People Earn Less

Everyone is a little afraid of the job market these days. But young people especially have a lot to fear. They generally have a hard time finding a job; and when they do, it doesn't pay much. Entry-level wages in most jobs have declined since 1973.

Back then, high school graduates could expect to go to work for the equivalent of $8.56 an hour. By 1993, they could expect only $6.42, a decline of 25%. College graduates fare better, but not by much. Their entry-level jobs now pay 7% less than they did 20 years ago.

Opportunities for college graduates have been constricted by corporate downsizing. In 1993, the College Employment Research Institute reported that the job market for recent graduates was the poorest it had been since World War II, with at least 35% of graduates taking jobs not requiring a college education.

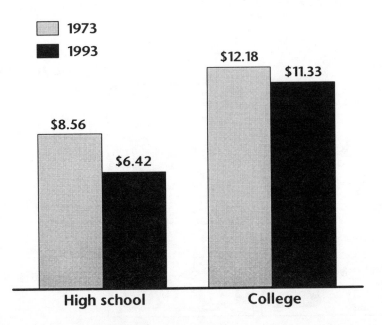

Entry-level wages for high school and college graduates ($1992)

- 1973
- 1993

High school: $8.56 (1973), $6.42 (1993)
College: $12.18 (1973), $11.33 (1993)

2.11 Jobless in 1994

There's an old saying: If your neighbor can't find a job, the economy is suffering a recession. But if you're the one who can't find a job, it's a depression.

Depression is fairly permanent for some groups. In 1994, the average unemployment rate for whites was about 5%. It was more than twice as high, at 12%, for African-Americans and 10% for Latinos.

Young people are especially vulnerable. Even for those ages 20 to 24, the unemployment rate was far above average.

People aren't counted among the unemployed unless they have no paying job, are able and willing to work, and are actively seeking employment.

In 1994, the official overall unemployment rate was 6%. But this leaves out "discouraged workers" (those who wanted a job but gave up looking) and those who are only "half employed" (working at part-time jobs because that's all they could find). When these workers are added, the jobless rate amounts to about 9%.

Individuals unemployed and seeking work as a percentage of the labor force, 1994

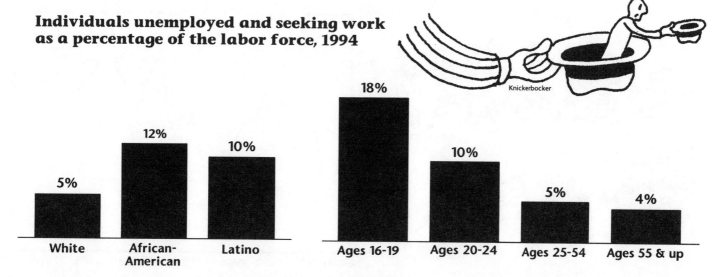

Knickerbocker

White — 5%
African-American — 12%
Latino — 10%

Ages 16-19 — 18%
Ages 20-24 — 10%
Ages 25-54 — 5%
Ages 55 & up — 4%

2.12 Unemployment Marches On

Unemployment rates move like a roller coaster with the business cycle. They go up when economic growth slows, down when it picks up. The problem is, they don't come down as much as they used to.

Until about 1974, unemployment averaged about 5%. Then it began to increase, with sharp peaks in 1975 and 1982. Now, even in periods of economic growth, like 1994, unemployment remains relatively high.

Being out of work is hard on people. Statistical studies show that it contributes to problems like alcoholism, child abuse, and mental illness. Unemployment also means that the economy is functioning below its potential. Putting more people to work can increase output and growth.

Unemployment rate, 1950-94
(unemployed as a percentage of the civilian labor force)

Russell Christian

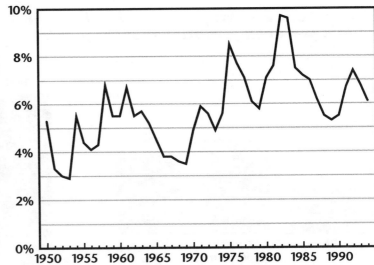

2.13 Surprise Layoffs

In 1990 and 1991, about 1.4 millions workers lost jobs as a result of plant closings or layoffs.

Advance notice helps workers adjust to job loss. In 1988, Congress enacted the Worker Adjustment and Retraining Act, which requires large employers to provide advance notice under certain conditions. The act has not been very effective, however:

A General Accounting Office analysis of a sample of layoffs in 1990 shows that about 47% of layoffs affecting 250 or more workers were exempt from advance notice requirements because they did not affect one third or more of the employees at the work site.

Only 50% of employers provided advance notice, even where it was required by law.

2.14 Unemployment Elsewhere

Need a job? Perhaps you could emigrate to Japan. Unemployment rates there have long remained under 3%. So much for the argument that high unemployment rates are an inevitable feature of advanced industrial economies.

The U.S. isn't the only country in which unemployment is on the rise. Our rates have actually stayed below those of Great Britain and Canada, where slow economic growth has limited job creation. Even Germany has suffered some setbacks in this respect.

But economic policy, as well as growth rates, plays an important role. Germany has made concerted—and successful—efforts to lower unemployment with apprenticeship, job training, and referral programs.

Efforts to promote faster growth by lowering interest rates could help bring unemployment down in both Europe and the U.S.

Unemployment trends in major industrial economies
(adjusted to approximate U.S. definitions)

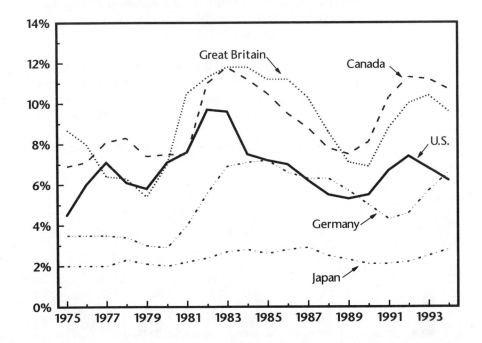

2.15 The Decline of Union Membership

More workers in this country used to carry union cards. The number of members has declined steadily as a percentage of all employees, from over 30% in 1954 to about 16% in 1993.

Until 1980, unions grew in membership despite a decrease in their percentage share. But between 1980 and 1984, they lost 2.7 million members, partly because recessions in those years led to job losses.

But there is another reason for the decline. Employers' resistance to unionization has grown. Formal complaints against unfair labor practices (such as firing union organizers) more than doubled between 1970 and 1980. Threats to close down and move overseas have also undermined union efforts.

Unionized employees as a percentage of all employees, 1950-93

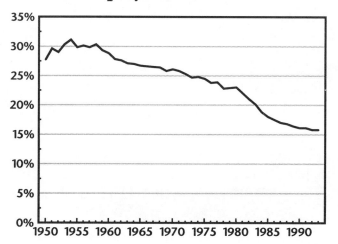

2.16 Who Belongs to Unions?

The common caricature of a union member is a white male factory worker wearing a hard hat. But the face of unions in this country has changed. African-Americans are well represented, with a higher percentage (21%) than either whites or Latinos. Women are almost as likely as men to belong: 13% compared with 18% of all employed men.

The types of places where union members work have also changed. Manufacturing remains much more heavily unionized than most services, but many industrial jobs have been lost through downsizing and restructuring. On the other hand, many campaigns to organize public-sector workers have proved successful. A large percentage of teachers and police are unionized.

U.S. labor law makes life difficult for union organizers, but many are busy persuading clerks, secretaries, and other service workers to join up.

Percentage of all employees in various groups belonging to unions in 1993

Women
13%

Men
18%

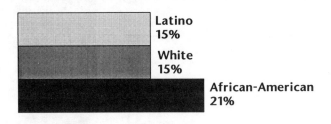

Latino
15%

White
15%

African-American
21%

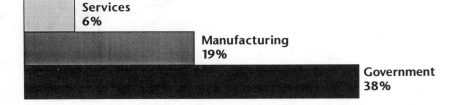

Services
6%

Manufacturing
19%

Government
38%

Chapter 3 **Women**

Russell Christian

"**Y**ou haven't come a very long way, baby." Imagine the woman's gentle voice, as the camera focuses on a flattering angle of a man struggling to vacuum a rug. You probably won't see it on television, but it would be a good antidote to the ads you do see. And it's a reminder that both men and women have a long way to go to achieve an economy with a fair division of labor between the sexes. How has women's place in the economy changed in recent years? As *Chart 3.1* shows, most women now earn a wage. But they often pay a high price in reduced leisure time because they continue to do most of the housework and child care. Statistics are hard to come by, but *Chart 3.2* describes the allocation of nonmarket work among employed men and women.

Women's traditional household responsibilities have always influenced the type of paid work they were allowed or encouraged to undertake. In recent years, many women have moved into well-paying professional jobs once monopolized by men, as seen in *Chart 3.3*. On the other hand, as *Chart 3.4* points out, most women workers remain in sex-typed and low-paid pink-collar jobs.

There is some good news. Women have narrowed the gender wage gap. *Chart 3.5* documents substantial improvements in the relative earnings of full-time women wage earners across all racial/ethnic groups. But equally qualified women should earn exactly what men earn. Many statistical studies reveal that they don't; as *Chart 3.6* shows, they earn less than men do even in jobs that require substantial educational credentials, such as computer programming and the law.

International comparisons in *Chart 3.7* show that the U.S. is in something of a middle position among industrialized countries in terms of gender equality. Women in Japan earn far less relative to men, while women in Australia earn more, largely as a result of public policies that support pay equity. *Chart 3.8* makes a case for more attention to the low levels of pay in traditionally female jobs. Many women don't seem to be paid the true worth of their work.

The transformation of American families has had a huge impact on women. Married-couple families still make up a majority of households. But as *Chart 3.9* shows, their importance is shrinking. Women maintain a growing percentage of all households and an even faster growing percentage of all families with one or more children under age 18 (see *Chart 3.10*). This demographic shift has been accompanied by other salient trends. As *Chart 3.11* documents, many fathers fail to contribute adequately to the support of their children. The economic burden on mothers has increased even as the scope for reproductive choice has diminished. *Chart 3.12* describes the impact of cutbacks in public funding.

Motherhood now poses a huge economic risk for women. Over half of all families living in poverty are maintained by women alone, a significant increase since 1959, as *Chart 3.13* shows. Yet public support for these families has declined, and the political mood has shifted toward policies that blame the victims. *Chart 3.14* outlines some of the myths and realities of welfare reform.

Even mothers with adequate incomes struggle to find decent, affordable childcare that would enable them to better combine work and family responsibilities. *Chart 3.15* points to the growing importance of organized childcare centers. What could U.S. policy do to improve public support for child rearing? *Chart 3.16* shows that many European countries, especially France, set a good example.

3.1 Most Women Earn a Wage

Every year, more women bring home a paycheck. For more than a century, women's work has been shifting from the home to the factory, shop, and office. Since 1979, more than half of women over age 16 have been working or looking for work in the paid labor force.

Black women have, until recently, been more likely than others to work for pay, largely because of the legacy of slavery, discrimination, and low family income. Today, however, there is little difference in the labor force participation of women by race because white women entered paid employment at a particularly rapid rate in the last few years.

Mothers are the fastest-growing group within the labor force. By 1993, 60% of married women with children under 6 were in the labor force, although a much smaller percentage worked full-time.

Labor force participation rates for women
(age 16 and up)

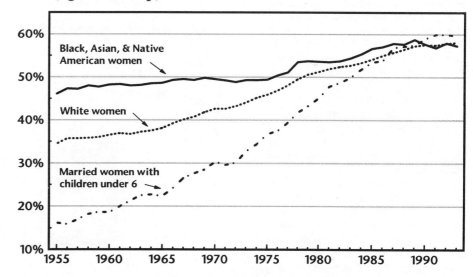

Black, Asian, & Native American women

White women

Married women with children under 6

3.2 Who Does the Housework?

A woman's work is never done. In fact, there may be more of it than ever. Despite their increasing participation in the labor force, employed women do about 38 hours of housework a week on average, compared with 22 hours for employed men. Much of the difference is explained by women's work as mothers. The addition of 2 or more children to a household almost doubles a woman's hours of household work, from 28 to 51 hours per week. Men actually do less household work when there are 2 or more children than when there is only 1.

Some male partners do their share of cooking, cleaning, and diaper changing, but not very many. In 1987, employed husbands did only 32% as much household work as their employed wives.

The time-budget studies that provide such information are not very current or reliable. If more economists did housework, they might collect more data on it. A bill introduced into Congress in 1992 by Representative Barbara Rose Collins of Michigan would require the Bureau of Labor Statistics to conduct regular time-use studies and include estimates of the value of housework in the gross domestic product.

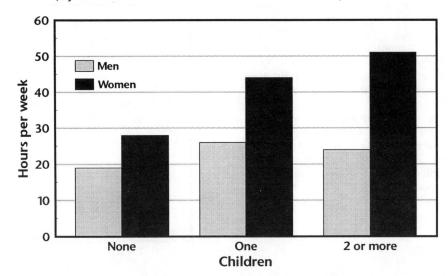

Average hours of household work per week for employed men and women, 1987
(by number of children in the household)

3.3 Nice Work If You Can Get It

More women are climbing the professional/managerial job ladder. In the 1950s and 1960s, they were often blocked from entering fields such as engineering and medicine. But in the 1970s, a militant women's movement helped open the door. Affirmative action programs were particularly effective at improving women's opportunities to pursue advanced educational degrees.

By 1993, women accounted for 9% of all engineers, 22% of all lawyers and judges, 43% of all managers, and 21% of all doctors. In some ways, this trend has strengthened the women's movement by putting more women into positions of power. But it has also increased income inequality, intensifying the impact of class and race differences upon efforts to organize around gender issues.

Nice work if you can get it, but you can't always get it just by trying. It helps to come from a family that can pay the bills for college and graduate school.

Women in professions
(as a percentage of total in these occupations)

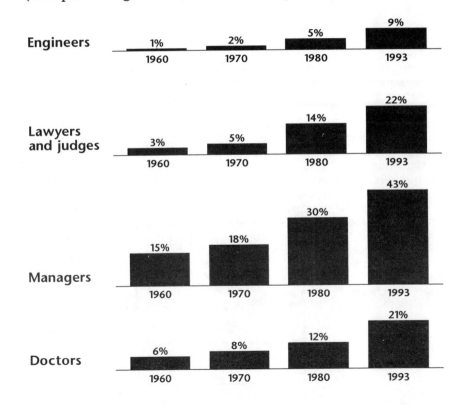

Engineers
1% 1960 2% 1970 5% 1980 9% 1993

Lawyers and judges
3% 1960 5% 1970 14% 1980 22% 1993

Managers
15% 1960 18% 1970 30% 1980 43% 1993

Doctors
6% 1960 8% 1970 12% 1980 21% 1993

3.4 Pink-collar Jobs

Women have specialized in jobs that don't fit the traditional blue-collar/white-collar distinction, jobs that require caring for other people. They represent the overwhelming majority of workers in jobs such as nursing, teaching, secretarial, and personal service. Within more detailed occupational categories, segregation is often even more extreme. In 1993, for instance, women represented 97% of all child care workers in private homes.

Such occupational segregation puts women at an economic disadvantage. The greater the number of women relative to men in an occupation, the lower the average pay. No wonder many describe women's jobs as a pink-collar ghetto.

Women as a percentage of all employees in selected occupations, 1993

Nurses and other health-assessment and treating jobs	86%
Teachers (except college and university)	75%
Secretaries and other administrative support	79%
Hairdressers and other personal service occupations	81%

STUDIES SHOW THAT WOMEN WITH "SEXY" NAMES LIKE DAWN AND CHERYL ARE...

LESS LIKELY TO BE PROMOTED TO MANAGERIAL JOBS THAN WOMEN WITH NAMES LIKE...

BILL OR ROGER.

Nicole Hollander

3.5 Women Still Earn Less Than Men

Women are gaining on men. Over the past 12 years, they have substantially improved their economic position. But in 1992, women still earned only about 71 cents for every dollar a man earned.

For a long time, women's relative earnings were stuck at about 60% of men's. Things began to change when they fought their way into advanced education and better-paying jobs. Also, women were less affected than men by the loss of well-paying manufacturing jobs in the 1980s. Because men's earnings increased hardly at all between 1979 and 1992, a modest increase in women's earnings had a big impact.

The difference between women's and men's wages is greatest among whites. Because African-Americans and Latinos earn less overall, women in those groups earned more relative to men in 1992: 89% and 86%, respectively, compared to 70% for whites.

Women's earnings as a percentage of men's
(year-round, full-time workers)

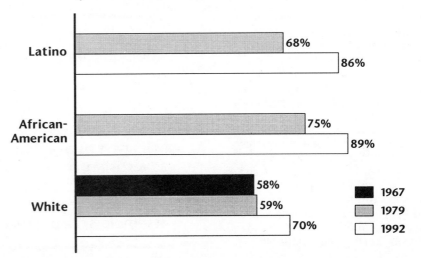

Latino
- 68%
- 86%

African-American
- 75%
- 89%

White
- 58%
- 59%
- 70%

■ 1967
▨ 1979
□ 1992

3.6 Equal Work, Unequal Pay

More than 20 years ago, the Equal Pay Act made it illegal to pay women less for doing the same work as men. Of course, in most cases, they don't do the same work, so the law is difficult to enforce. That's why most of women's gains have come from entering new, traditionally male occupations.

Even within the same occupation, however, pay differentials are glaring: female computer programmers and lawyers earn significantly less than males in those jobs. Some, but not all, of this disparity is explained by differences in age and experience on the job. Within occupations, women are often segregated in the specialties that pay the least.

Many women don't know, and aren't allowed to ask, how much they earn relative to men in their workplace. It is risky and expensive to sue an employer, and the Equal Employment Opportunity Commission can help only a small number of people.

Several recent lawsuits have vindicated women who were willing to fight for their rights. In the largest civil rights case settlement in history, State Farm Insurance agreed, in April 1992, to pay women employees $157 million in compensation for practices that had excluded them from the job of sales agent. More recently, Lucky Supermarkets, accused of segregating women in its delicatessen and bakery departments and discouraging them from management training programs, agreed to pay $75 million in damages and $20 million to support affirmative action programs.

Women's median wages for selected jobs as a percentage of men's median wages for the same jobs, 1992

Computer programmers	**84%**
Lawyers	**78%**
Managers of marketing, advertising, public relations	**69%**
Machine operators, assemblers, inspectors	**68%**

3.7 Comparable Worth

Are women workers paid what they are worth? Jobs can be ranked into comparable categories according to their requirements (such as educational level) and characteristics (such as level of responsibility). Studies differ, but they usually show that women are paid far less than men for comparable jobs.

For instance, a secretary (usually a woman) requires as much education and takes as much responsibility as a carpenter (usually a man) but is paid far less.

In the 1980s, 20 states implemented pay equity programs that reduced the gender wage gap. Minnesota, Oregon, and Washington were among the most successful. Unions also play an active role in pressing for pay equity: Collective bargaining has convinced some municipalities (including the city of Los Angeles) to change relative pay scales.

Knickerbocker

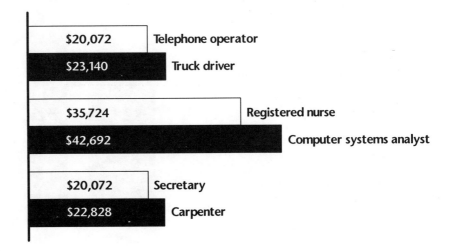

Annual earnings in comparable occupations in 1993

$20,072	Telephone operator
$23,140	Truck driver
$35,724	Registered nurse
$42,692	Computer systems analyst
$20,072	Secretary
$22,828	Carpenter

3.8 Women's Wages Around the World

Women Down Under take the cake. In Australia, women earn more relative to men (91%) than in any other country reporting to the International Labour Organisation in Geneva. One reason is the pay equity policy adopted by the Australian government in the 1970s. Employers have been pressured to increase wages in women's jobs.

Women fare slightly better in many European countries than in the U.S., partly because there is less overall inequality in wages there and more women belong to unions. In Germany, women earn about 79% of what their male counterparts earn. Though comparable statistics are hard to come by, Scandinavian women probably enjoy even more equality than German women.

In Japan, on the other hand, public policies discourage married women from working and do little to combat other forms of discrimination. As a result, Japanese women earn little more than half of what men earn.

Women's wages as a percentage of men's wages, 1991
(average hourly or median weekly earnings in nonagricultural employment)

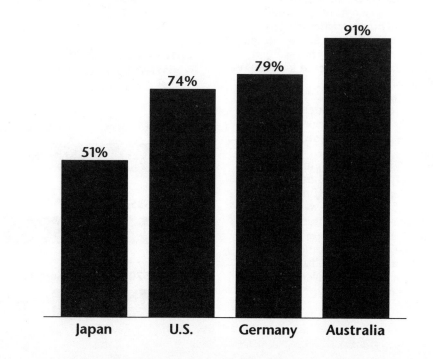

3.9 Married-Couple Families Are Less Common

om, Dad, Buddy, and Sue aren't as likely to live together as they once were. They may all have their own apartments. In 1950, almost 80% of all U.S. households were married-couple families. By 1993, less than 60% of households fit this description. And less than half of these included children under 18.

More and more individuals, including the elderly, are choosing to live by themselves. Single-person households increased from 9% to 25% of all households between 1950 and 1993. The percentage of all households that are families maintained by women also increased, from 8% to 12%.

Getting married is still popular. But the amount of time that men and women stay married has gone down as the divorce rate has risen. In 1993, only a little more than half of all women over 15 were married and living with their husbands.

Changes in household structure were particularly rapid in the 1970s and 1980s and may now be slowing down. But with incomes declining and rents going up, Buddy and Sue may soon find that they can't afford to live away from home.

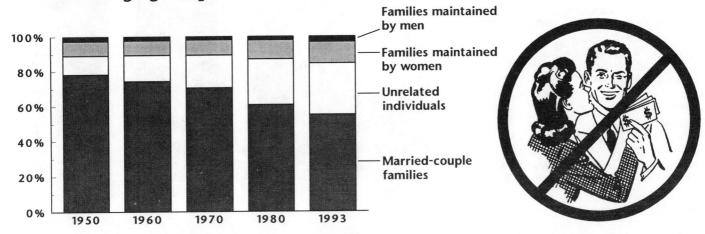

The changing composition of households

Families maintained by men

Families maintained by women

Unrelated individuals

Married-couple families

100%, 80%, 60%, 40%, 20%, 0%

1950 1960 1970 1980 1993

3.10 More Families Are Maintained by Women

The Census Bureau used to define a female-headed family as one in which there was "no man present in the home." In 1980, however, the bureau dispensed with its patriarchal assumption that any man present must be a household head, substituted the concept of "householder," and let people designate their own.

Whatever words you use to describe it, a growing percentage of families are maintained by women alone. In 1993, 22% of all families with 1 or more children under 18 fell into this category.

This trend is even more pronounced among young families. More than 49% of all families with young children headed by a person under age 25 were maintained by women in 1993.

Look at it from a child's point of view: In 1993, more than 1 out of 4 children lived with only 1 parent. And 88% of these lived with their mothers.

Families with children maintained by women
(as percentage of all families with 1 or more children under age 18)

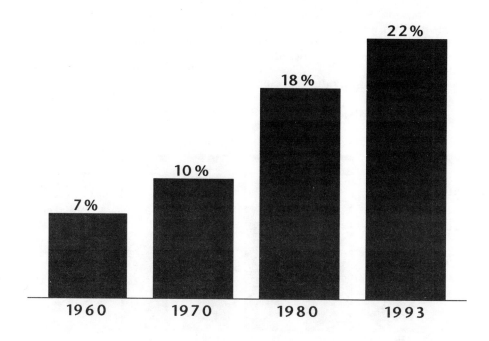

1960	1970	1980	1993
7%	10%	18%	22%

3.11 Deadbeat Dads

In 1992, child support enforcement agencies were able to collect only one-quarter of what absent parents (predominantly fathers) owed.

In 1989, almost 10 million women were living with children under age 21 whose fathers were absent from the home.

Only 50% of these women were awarded child support payments due the same year (compared with 48% in 1981).

Only 51% of those due payments received the full amount (compared with 47% in 1981).

Child support payments have not kept pace with inflation. The real value of child support payments made by fathers who do not reside with their children has fallen since 1969.

A recent Census Bureau study found that among families where the children remained with the mother after the parents separated, the poverty rate jumped from 19% to 36%.

Russell Christian

3.12 Reproductive Rights and Wrongs

Many women, especially teens, lack access to forms of contraception other than condoms, which require male cooperation. Yet total public dollars spent for contraceptive services in the U.S. fell by one-third between 1980 and 1990.

The number of abortions performed every year is about 40% of the number of live births. Yet many poor women find abortions difficult to obtain. Since 1976, the Hyde Amendment has banned federal funding for abortions. More than 30% of all women of childbearing age live in counties with no identifiable abortion facilities.

The cost of prenatal care for a pregnant woman for 9 months is $600. The cost of medical care for a premature baby for 1 day is $2,500. The cost of drug treatment for a drug-addicted mother for 9 months is $5,000. The cost of medical care for a drug-exposed baby for 20 days is $30,000.

Russell Christian

3.13 Mothers, Children, and Poverty

Mothers on their own have always been particularly vulnerable to poverty, but over the past 25 years, their situation has worsened. Their families represented 52% of those with incomes below the poverty level in 1992, a slight increase from 48% in 1976.

This feminization of poverty reflects, in part, the pauperization of motherhood. Support from both fathers and the state has diminished in recent years, increasing the economic burden on mothers. Raising the next generation of workers and taxpayers is not considered productive work.

Nor does this country worry much about the final product. Over 65% of children living in African-American or Latino families maintained by women alone suffer the deprivations of poverty.

Percentage of all poor families maintained by women alone

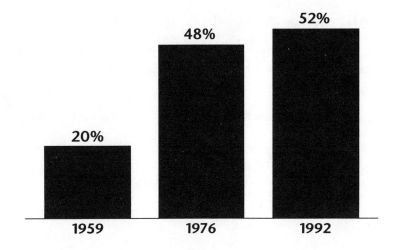

1959	1976	1992
20%	48%	52%

3.14 Welfare Myths and Realities

Myth: *Higher welfare benefits cause increases in the number of families maintained by women alone.*
Reality: Studies show no correlation between the level of benefits provided by Aid to Families with Dependent Children (AFDC) and the prevalence of female-headed families, either over time or across states.

Myth: *Since most mothers work outside the home, it is only fair to expect those without husbands to support themselves.*
Reality: While the majority of married mothers with children work for pay, most work only part-time or part-year. Is it reasonable to require AFDC mothers, who are solely responsible for child rearing, to work full-time?

Myth: *So-called workfare measures would save taxpayers money.*
Reality: Finding jobs and providing child care for mothers currently receiving welfare would require substantial increases in public spending.

Myth: *If welfare mothers would just find a job, they would be better off.*
Reality: Many welfare mothers already work for pay to supplement the low level of benefits they receive. Many of the jobs available to them pay less than poverty-level wages, and child care is costly and difficult to find.

3.15 The Demand for Child Care

Good child care is hard to find. As more women with young children enter the labor force, parents rely more and more on organized child care facilities. In 1991, 23% of all working women with children under age 5 relied on such facilities, compared with 13% in 1977.

In many areas, the demand for child care is much greater than the supply, waiting lists are long, and costs are prohibitive. Often, the non-affluent need not apply: Low-income families spend more than 20% of their income on child care, about what they spend on housing.

Furthermore, parents don't always know what kind of care their children are getting. Few federal regulations govern child care centers, and turnover rates are high among staff, who typically earn even less than waitresses or hairdressers.

"THE BOSS SAYS OUR DEMAND IS WAY AHEAD OF ITS TIME!"

Percentage of working women with a child under 5 using organized child care facilities

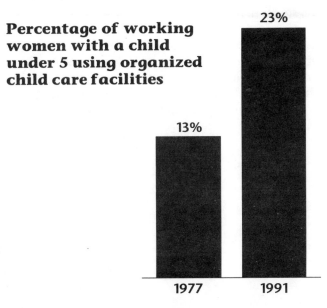

3.16 Family Policies in Europe

Paid family leave of more than 12 weeks is guaranteed by most countries of Western Europe. The U.S. currently requires public and private employers with 50 or more workers to grant employees as much as 12 weeks of unpaid leave for the birth or adoption of a child, to care for an ill family member, or to recover from their own serious illness. Only about 66% of the workforce is covered (the rest work for small firms).

Child care in the U.S. is often expensive and difficult to find. By contrast, in France, 99% of 3-, 4-, and 5-year-olds attend preschools at no or minimal charge. Excellent daycare facilities for younger children are heavily subsidized by the government.

Family allowances (regular payments to help support children) are offered by most countries of Western Europe. The U.S. allows parents to deduct money from their taxable income for children as dependents. But the value of this deduction as a percentage of family income has declined over time. Tripling the current deduction would restore the relative value it had in 1948.

Poverty rates among families maintained by women alone are far lower in Western Europe than in the United States. The same is true of poverty rates among children.

Chapter 4 **People of Color**

Russell Christian

"**D**emocracy," emphasizes the Reverend Jesse Jackson, "doesn't guarantee success—it guarantees opportunity." What kinds of economic opportunities do people of color have in this country? They are more likely than whites to die in infancy, grow up in poverty, attend poor schools, and experience unemployment. While racial discrimination isn't nearly as fierce as it used to be, it still has a sharp bite.

The charts in this chapter document the growing racial and ethnic diversity of the population, the economic gains experienced since the Civil Rights Act of 1964, and the reversals of the 1980s.

Chart 4.1 describes the components of the U.S. population in 1994, while *Chart 4.2* examines the ethnic diversity of Latinos and Asian and Pacific Islanders in more detail. Not as many government statistics are collected on Native Americans, but *Chart 4.3* presents some important facts about their situation. Recent immigration to the U.S. is described in *Chart 4.4*, which also discusses some of the economic consequences.

African-Americans and Latinos have incomes considerably lower than whites, and the disparities have changed remarkably little over time (see *Chart 4.5*). One consequence of inequality, examined in *Chart 4.6*, is a greater susceptibility to poverty. Between 1959 and 1975, both economic growth and social programs helped reduce poverty rates. Between 1975 and 1992, however, rates went up for all groups.

Low incomes are partly due to lack of jobs. When the overall unemployment rate increased in the early 1980s, it increased even more for African-American and Latino workers. As *Chart 4.7* shows, the unemployment rate for the former runs about twice that of whites, with Latinos in between. This can't be explained away by differences in level of education attained. African-American college graduates were more likely to be unemployed in 1993 than white high school graduates (*Chart 4.8*).

African-Americans and Latinos are more likely than whites to work in dead-end jobs. *Chart 4.9* shows that they are overrepresented in less-skilled service occupations and underrepresented in managerial and professional jobs. In general, the public sector has offered African-Americans better opportunities than the private sector. As *Chart 4.10* shows, they enjoy both higher wages and a larger share of employment in state and local government than in the private sector.

In recent years, racial wage inequality has increased. African-Americans and Latinos now earn less relative to whites than they did in 1979 (*Chart 4.11*). Part of the explanation lies in the effects of industrial restructuring and deunionization, which had a particularly negative effect on African-American men (*Chart 4.12*). A political backlash against affirmative action, including complaints about "reverse discrimination," has also had an important impact. Yet recent studies using "testers" (matched pairs of job applicants who differ only by race) have uncovered evidence of persistent discrimination against African-Americans and Latinos (*Chart 4.13*).

Racial and ethnic disparities in educational attainment at both the high school and the college levels are pictured in *Chart 4.14*. People of color have suffered disproportionately from social policies that have had an adverse impact on children simply because they have larger families. Many children live in families maintained by women alone, where they are particularly susceptible to poverty (see *Charts 4.15* and *4.16*).

Most metropolitan areas are highly segregated by race. *Chart 4.17* shows that the percentage of African-Americans who would have to move to a different neighborhood in order to achieve desegregation has declined only slightly since 1970. Here again, "testers" have provided concrete evidence of discrimination.

People of color also face unfair obstacles when they try to buy a home. *Chart 4.18* tallies mortgage denial rates by race and ethnicity and summarizes a study showing that discriminatory patterns persist, even when differences in income and credit history are taken into account.

4.1 Who We Are

The U.S. has traditionally been described as a melting pot, but a better metaphor might be a salad bowl. In 1995, about a quarter of the population had ethnic backgrounds that set them apart from the culturally and politically dominant white population.

African-Americans and Latinos accounted for 12% and 10% of the population. Asians and Pacific Islanders made up about 3%, and Native Americans nearly 1%. Because these groups are concentrated in certain geographic areas, they often represent a much larger percentage of the population in their own communities.

All these groups are growing faster than the white population. Ethnic diversity is here to stay.

Racial and ethnic composition of the U.S. population, 1995
(resident population, middle-series projection)

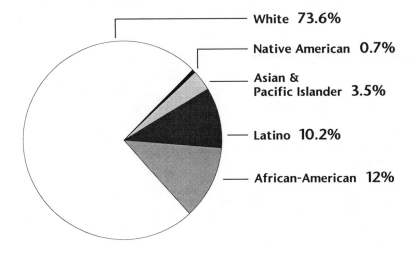

White **73.6%**

Native American **0.7%**

Asian & Pacific Islander **3.5%**

Latino **10.2%**

African-American **12%**

4.2 Asian and Latino Diversity

Many people strongly identify with their families' nation of origin. The broad ethnic categories used by the Census Bureau conceal enormous diversity, particularly among Latinos and Asians or Pacific Islanders.

Individuals with a Mexican heritage represented 60% of the Latino population in 1990, concentrated largely in the Southwest, where many have lived for generations. Puerto Ricans are the second-largest category, followed by Cubans and by those from other countries of Central or South America, many of whom are recent immigrants.

Among Asians or Pacific Islanders, Chinese and Filipinos are the most numerous. Most Japanese and Chinese have long been citizens of this country, and Hawaiians are native to this country. Other groups include many recent immigrants.

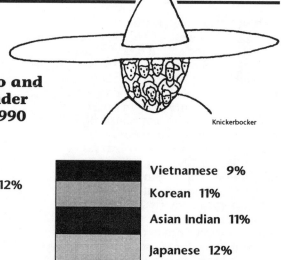

Knickerbocker

Components of Latino and Asian or Pacific Islander ethnic categories in 1990

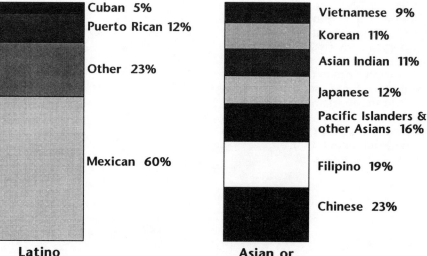

Cuban 5%
Puerto Rican 12%

Other 23%

Mexican 60%

Latino

Vietnamese 9%

Korean 11%

Asian Indian 11%

Japanese 12%

Pacific Islanders & other Asians 16%

Filipino 19%

Chinese 23%

Asian or Pacific Islander

4.3 Native Americans

About 1,959,000 individuals, or 0.8% of the population, identified themselves as American Indian, Eskimo, or Aleut in 1990 (an increase from 0.6% in 1980).

The largest American Indian tribes are Cherokee (16.4% of the total), Navajo (11.7%), Chippewa (5.5%), Sioux (5.5%), and Choctaw (4.4%).

Only about 38%, primarily the young and elderly, lived on reservations, trust lands, or other "identified areas." Many Native Americans of working age sought employment elsewhere.

In 1989, about 31% of Native Americans had incomes under the poverty line, many of them among the poorest of the poor.

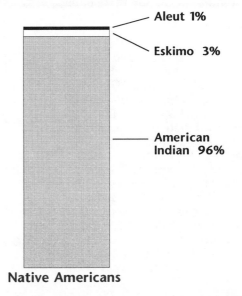

Aleut 1%

Eskimo 3%

American Indian 96%

Native Americans

4.4 Immigration on the Rise

The Statue of Liberty has watched over many waves of immigration to this country. New entrants increased substantially in the 1980s. But they still represented a much smaller share of the total population than in earlier periods of American history.

Do immigrants use up more public money than they pay in taxes? Studies show that immigrants who entered this country before 1980 now have an average household income higher than that of native-born Americans and contribute more to government budgets. Undocumented workers are not officially eligible for benefits, and even legal immigrants are effectively prohibited from receiving most forms of public assistance for 3 to 5 years after arrival.

But recent immigrants, particularly refugees from Vietnam and Russia, are quite susceptible to poverty. One problem is that states and counties often pay the cost of helping them out, even though the federal government collects most of the taxes they pay.

Legal immigration by area of origin, 1951-90 (millions)

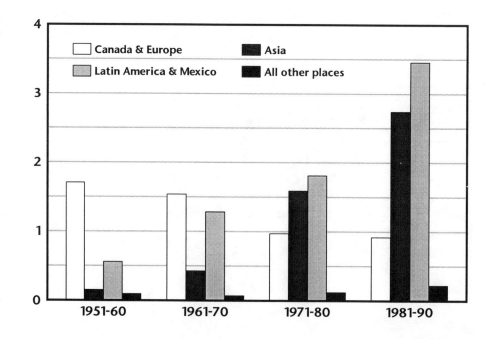

4.5 Lower Family Income

Knickerbocker

Class and color go together in the United States. Most African-American and Latino families must get by on far less income than white families. And despite some improvements in the mid-1980s, their inflation-adjusted incomes were still lower in 1992 than they were in 1978.

The Cosby Show notwithstanding, few families of color enjoy an upper-middle-class standard of living. Only 12% of African-American households and 15% of Latino households had incomes over $50,000 in 1992, compared with 27% of white households.

Differences in income over several generations result in even greater differences in wealth. In 1991, Latino and African-American families had a median net worth of about a tenth that of white families.

Median family income, by race and Latino origin

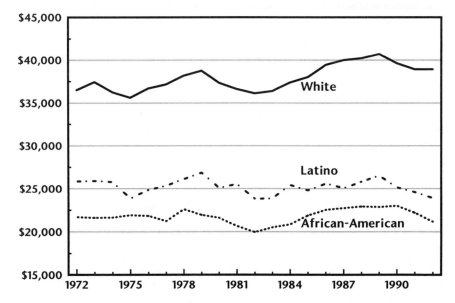

4.6 The Color of Poverty

Many people consider poverty somebody else's problem, and racism makes it easier to blame the victims for laziness or immorality. But the history and structure of the economy show that poverty is a systemic problem. Inherited inequalities, discrimination, unemployment, and rips in the social safety net have left African-Americans and Latinos more susceptible than whites.

For a while, things were getting better. Between 1959 and 1975, government antipoverty programs and relatively low unemployment rates decreased the overall poverty rate and reduced the differences in poverty rates among ethnic groups.

But after 1975, these trends were reversed. Unemployment went up, and cuts in federal social spending had a particularly ugly impact on people of color. Public support for families with dependent children declined, leaving many kids vulnerable to squalor and violence. In 1992, more than 40% of African-American and Latino children lived in poverty.

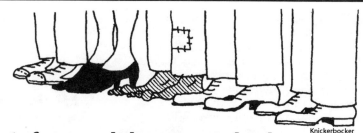

Knickerbocker

Percent of persons below poverty level, by race and Latino origin

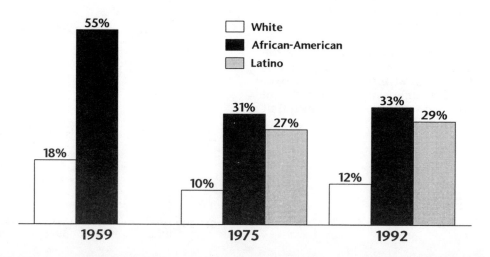

Legend: White, African-American, Latino

1959: White 18%, African-American 55%
1975: White 10%, African-American 31%, Latino 27%
1992: White 12%, African-American 33%, Latino 29%

4.7 Last Hired

High unemployment rates afflict African-Americans and Latinos more than whites. In 1994, 11.8% of black workers and 10.2% of Latinos could not find jobs, while only 5.4% of whites were in the same predicament.

Teenagers had an even harder time. The unemployment rate among black youths was 36%; for whites, it was 16%.

Persistently high unemployment rates discourage people from looking for work. Black male labor force participation rates have dropped considerably in recent years.

When people of color bear a large share of the burden of unemployment, they buffer whites against the ups and downs of the business cycle.

Unemployment rate, by race and Latino origin
(civilian workers age 16 and above)

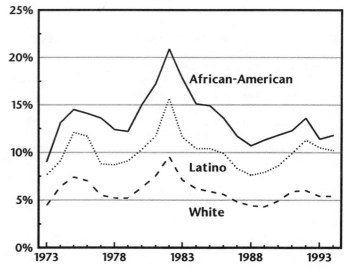

4.8 Unemployment by Degrees

A college diploma is worth at least its weight in gold these days. Those who hold one are much more likely to find a job and earn a decent wage.

But a diploma doesn't guarantee protection against unemployment or discrimination. Even with a college degree, African-Americans and Latinos had far higher unemployment rates than their white counterparts in 1993.

Perhaps some of them were considered "overqualified" for the jobs they applied for. If affirmative action was really leading to "reverse discrimination," as some critics argue, one would expect to see exactly the opposite pattern. The fact is, educated whites have an easier time finding jobs than any other ethnic group.

Youth unemployment, by educational attainment, 1993
(individuals ages 16-24)

	Diploma		
	None	High school	College
White	20%	11%	4%
African-American	34%	20%	12%
Latino	17%	15%	9%

4.9 More Menial Work

Historically, people of color have been confined to jobs whites wanted to avoid, like domestic service. Today, they work mostly in jobs that involve housekeeping for the economy as a whole, such as sweeping halls, preparing food, waiting on tables, and caring for children.

About a quarter of all African-Americans and a fifth of all Latinos work at the low end of the occupational ladder, in poorly paid service jobs. Not surprisingly, they are underrepresented in managerial and professional occupations. Only 18% of African-Americans and 14% of Latinos hold such jobs, compared with 27% of all white workers.

Knickerbocker

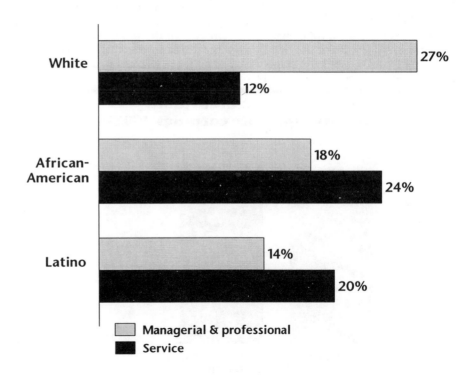

Employed civilians, by occupation, race, and Latino origin, 1993

White
27%
12%

African-American
18%
24%

Latino
14%
20%

Managerial & professional
Service

4.10 Public vs. Private Employment

Government has long provided better jobs to African-Americans than has the private sector. After 1950, the percentage of black workers in the public sector grew rapidly, peaking in the mid-1970s at about 24%. State and local employment has been particularly important. In 1991, blacks filled about 20% of these jobs, compared with 10% in the economy as a whole.

Antidiscrimination and affirmative action policies have had a bigger impact in the public sector, where they are more easily enforced. As a result, blacks earn substantially more relative to whites in state and local government (86%) than in all jobs (77%).

Budget cuts have led to reductions in state, local, and federal employment. The public sector no longer offers a wide avenue for advancement.

African-American earnings relative to white earnings, 1991

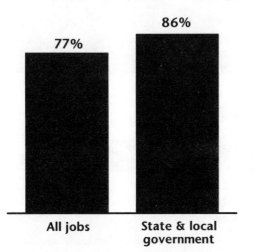

African-American share of employment, 1991

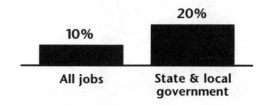

4.11 Wage Inequalities

Between 1979 and 1993, both men and women of color lost ground relative to whites of the same gender. African-American women saw their relative earnings decline from 93% to 86% of white women's, while Latino men's declined from 74% to 64% of white men's.

This represented the reversal of a long-standing trend. Between 1956 and 1976, blacks, Asians, and Native American workers (all labeled "non-white" by the Census Bureau) narrowed the gap between their earnings and those of white workers.

Increased racial inequality reflected the growing pay gap between less educated and more educated workers. But cutbacks in government jobs and a weakened commitment to fighting racial discrimination also played a part.

Median weekly earnings of African-Americans and Latinos as a percentage of those of whites

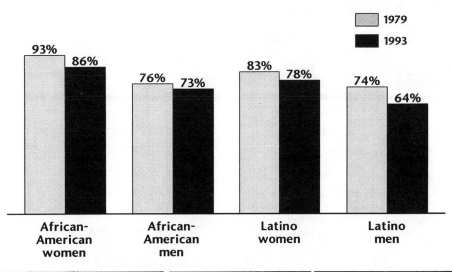

- 1979
- 1993

African-American women: 93% (1979), 86% (1993)
African-American men: 76% (1979), 73% (1993)
Latino women: 83% (1979), 78% (1993)
Latino men: 74% (1979), 64% (1993)

... AND NOW THE NEWS.

KONOPACKI

TELL ME SOMETHIN,' BABY. WHAT WOULD YOU LIKE TO BE WHEN YOU GROW UP?

A RICH WHITE MAN!

4.12 Deunionization Has Hurt African-Americans

African-Americans, once excluded from the trade union movement, have fought long and hard for collective bargaining rights. Ironically, just as they were beginning to enjoy some of the benefits, unions began going down the tubes.

Between 1979 and 1989, the percentage of African-Americans belonging to unions declined sharply because many union jobs were eliminated. The result was a significant loss of earnings for black female college graduates, as well as black high school graduates.

Because deunionization had a disproportionate impact on African-Americans, it contributed to increases in racial income inequality.

Impact of deunionization on changes in average hourly earnings of workers ages 25-64, 1979-89

	Percent belonging to unions		Effect of union decline on wages
	1979	1989	
African-American men			
High school dropout	42%	29%	-3%
High school graduate	56%	30%	-5%
College or more	41%	42%	0%
African-American women			
High school dropout	32%	18%	-2%
High school graduate	43%	24%	-2%
College or more	52%	28%	-5%

4.13 Affirmative Action

Statistical analysis shows that African-Americans and Latinos earn less than whites, even taking into account differences in education and labor force experience.

A recent study sent "testers" (carefully selected pairs of young black and white men matched closely in terms of education, work history, age, and height) to apply for entry-level jobs. The results: Blacks were 3 times more likely than whites to be rejected.

A similar study using matched pairs of Latino and Anglo men found that Latinos were significantly less likely to be offered a job interview or a job.

Facing a lawsuit backed by considerable evidence of discrimination against black customers and workers, Denny's Restaurants agreed to a settlement of $54 million in 1994. Shoney's Inc. and the Albertson's supermarket chain also recently settled racial discrimination suits.

4.14 The Education Gap Persists

Campus populations are turning noticeably paler. Racial and ethnic differences in education have always been greatest on the college level, and they intensified between 1980 and 1993.

Both African-Americans and Latinos have made significant progress in getting high school diplomas; but in 1993, less than 71% of those over age 25 had completed 4 or more years of high school. Less than 13% had completed 4 or more years of college. Cuts in aid for college students reinforced a decline in the percentage of low-income high school graduates going on to college. Budget cuts also shrank tutorial and counseling programs for disadvantaged students.

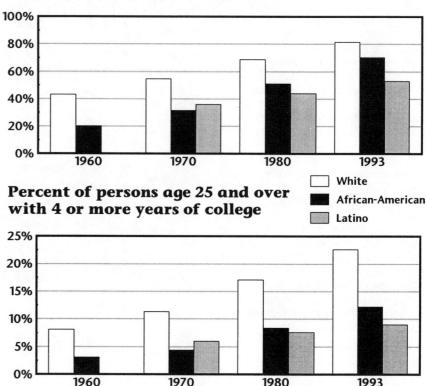

Percent of persons age 25 and over with 4 or more years of high school

Percent of persons age 25 and over with 4 or more years of college

☐ White
■ African-American
▨ Latino

4.15 Who's Raising the Kids?

African-American and Latino families have more kids. In 1993, fewer than half of all white families had any children under age 18, compared with 58% of African-American and 63% of Latino families.

All citizens depend on the future generation of workers to pay off public debt and provide support for the older generation through Social Security taxes. But public support for child rearing remains quite slim, and parenthood often leads to poverty.

The fact that many children are children of color may be one of the reasons why political priorities have shifted away from programs that benefit children, such as welfare, public education, and job training.

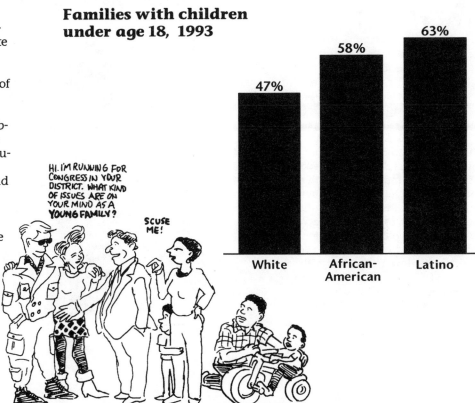

Families with children under age 18, 1993

White	African-American	Latino
47%	58%	63%

Howard Saunders

4.16 Many Women of Color Maintain Families

Mothers on their own are forced to cope with the triple burden of paying the bills, doing the housework, and looking after the kids. The proportion of families maintained by women alone has increased among all ethnic groups but is especially high among people of color. In 1993, 47% of African-American families and 23% of all Latino families fell in this category.

Some policy makers argue that public assistance programs have promoted female headship. But such programs vary considerably across states, and the percentage of families maintained by women is not significantly lower in states with low benefits. Also, female headship has increased significantly among affluent as well as poor families.

Families maintained by women alone, 1993

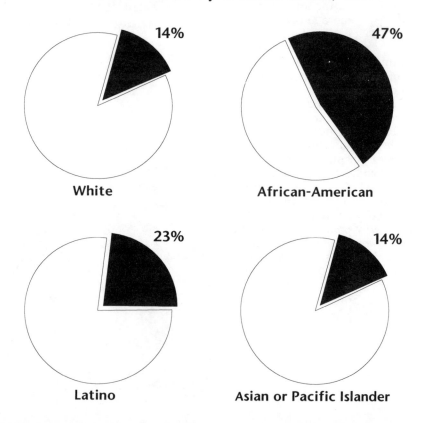

14%

White

47%

African-American

23%

Latino

14%

Asian or Pacific Islander

4.17 Segregation in Slow Decline

Ghettos are not going away. Most African-Americans live in highly segregated neighborhoods in large metropolitan areas. Over 65% would have to move in order to achieve desegregation.

This pattern reflects both the legacy and the ongoing practice of racial discrimination. Major court cases have revealed explicit segregation policies in public housing programs. "Testers" (individuals identical in every respect but their race) sent out to rent housing have exposed widespread discrimination in the private market.

Segregation is remarkably resistant to change, especially in Northern cities such as Chicago and New York. In the top 30 metropolitan areas as a whole, the segregation index declined only slightly between 1970 and 1990, and most of that change came in the earlier decade.

Percentage of African-Americans who would have to change their neighborhood of residence in order to achieve desegregation

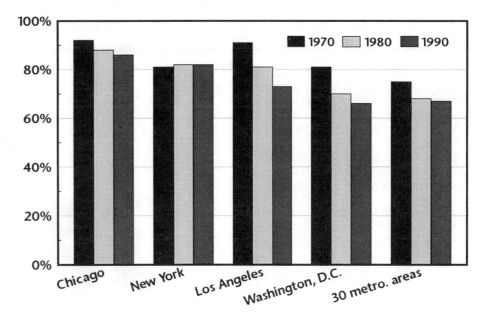

4.18 Banks Discriminate

"**B**ut most of those people don't really want to borrow money—and those who do have a terrible credit history." That's the explanation bankers initially gave when systematic differences in lending to whites, Latinos, and African-Americans were revealed. Then the Federal Reserve Bank of Boston performed a detailed statistical analysis of mortgage applications. It found that even if black and Latino borrowers had the same characteristics as whites (except for race), they were 56% more likely to be denied a mortgage.

It seems that few loan applicants have a flawless credit history, and most need some advice and the benefit of the doubt in order to get their loan. Predominantly white loan officers are most likely to extend such generosity to people who look and act like them.

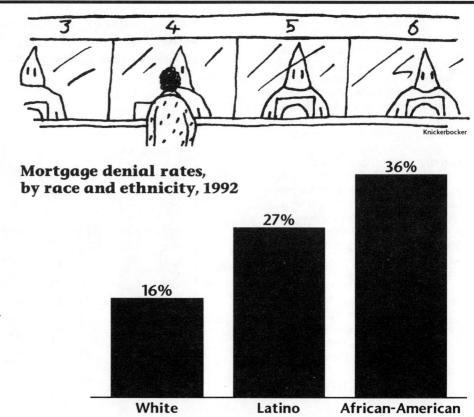

Knickerbocker

Mortgage denial rates, by race and ethnicity, 1992

White: 16%
Latino: 27%
African-American: 36%

Chapter 5 **Government Spending**

Russell Christian

For the past 20 years, the politics of tax-and-spend has dominated public debate. Some policy makers denounce Big Government as the source of all our economic woes. But the real problem is Bad Government.

This chapter offers a critical perspective on government spending and taxation. The national debt reached its highest percentage of GDP during World War II and, as *Chart 5.1* illustrates, decreased afterward until 1981, when the Reagan administration took charge. *Chart 5.2* shows why: Lower taxes and higher expenditures in the 1980s created bigger budget deficits. The federal government was forced to borrow more money every year to pay its bills.

Government spending accounts for a large share of GDP, about 34% in 1993. But the U.S. doesn't seem out of line in this respect. Japan spends the same percentage, and Germany and other members of the Organization for Economic Cooperation and Development (OECD) spend even more (see *Chart 5.3*). The same countries, however, tax their citizens more aggressively (see *Chart 5.4*).

Like the U.S., other industrialized countries run deficits and accumulate debt. While too much indebtedness is risky and inefficient, it often makes sense for governments to borrow to invest in the future or help stabilize the economy, just as families borrow to buy a house or to pay unexpected bills.

A simple formula like "balancing the budget" can do more harm than good. As *Chart 5.5* emphasizes, government spending that promotes economic growth can help reduce both deficits and debt.

A look at the composition of federal spending helps explain the need to reduce debt. *Chart 5.6* shows that interest payments doubled from 7% to 14% of the federal budget between 1970 and 1992. Declines in military spending made possible by the end of the Vietnam War were largely counterbalanced by the combination of higher interest payments and greater expenditures on Social Security and Medicare. The share of social spending in the overall budget actually declined from 1980 to 1992.

Chart 5.7 takes a closer look at social spending programs, documenting cuts in the share of education, training, employment, natural resources, environment, and energy. Another important category of federal spending is money devoted to infrastructure, civilian research and development, and education and training. These are the kinds of public investments that could make deficit spending pay off. Yet, in recent years, they have declined (see *Chart 5.8*).

Whatever happened to the "peace dividend" that the end of the Cold War was supposed to provide? In 1992, the U.S. spent far more on its military than France, the United Kingdom, Germany, and Japan combined (see *Chart 5.9*).

Congress proved reluctant to make sharp cuts in military spending, in part because the recession of the early 1990s accentuated the fact that many industries depended on the military for support. *Chart 5.10* presents better strategies for beating swords into plowshares.

What about the tax side of the budget picture? *Chart 5.11* shows that personal and corporate income taxes now account for a much smaller share of total revenue than they did in 1960. Regressive Social Security taxes, which take a bigger bite out of low and middling wages than high ones, have increased in importance. *Chart 5.12* tracks the corporate income tax over time in more detail, showing that it represents a declining share of profits.

The next series focuses on the impact of the so-called tax cuts of the 1980s. *Chart 5.13* reveals that the top 1% of all families got a big break, while the federal tax rate on the bottom 80% of the population remained virtually unchanged. But federal taxes tell only part of the story. Over 68% of state and local tax revenue is raised from regressive taxes that extract a greater percentage of income from poor and middle-income families than from the rich (see *Chart 5.14*). Enormous government subsidies and tax breaks go to large corporations (see *Chart 5.15*).

Social Security is an entitlement based on its own system of taxes and benefits. Many beneficiaries assume that they receive approximately the value of what they put in. Not so. As *Chart 5.16* explains, the Social Security system transfers money from the working-age population to retirees, and many relatively affluent retirees enjoy the benefits of what amounts to a "welfare" payment. The elderly deserve public support, but the current Social Security system is neither fair nor efficient. As a result, it doesn't offer much security to today's workers.

5.1 Borrowed Money

Governments get into debt the same way ordinary people do, by spending more than they take in. The resulting shortfall is called a "deficit." The only way to make up the difference is to borrow money, or go into debt. Usually a deficit describes a shortfall in a given year, while debt is the accumulated sum of money borrowed over many years.

Total U.S. debt in 1994 was about $4.7 trillion. But the national debt was actually bigger, as a percentage of gross domestic product (GDP), in the aftermath of World War II. Between 1950 and 1981, vigorous economic growth and mild inflation contributed to high tax revenues and reduced the debt burden.

The relative size of the national debt grew rapidly in the 1980s and became a cause for some concern. But debt itself isn't necessarily bad. If it helps finance productive investments, it can pay off.

Federal debt as a percentage of GDP, 1950-95

5.2 Bigger Deficits

"This administration is committed to a balanced budget and ... we will fight to the last blow to achieve it by 1984." That's what President Reagan proclaimed upon taking office back in 1981. Ten years later, the deficit had grown from 2.6% to 4.8% of the GDP.

Most of the increase in the deficit between 1981 and 1992 resulted from Reagan-initiated tax cuts. Expenditures increased only slightly. While spending on social programs declined, it was more than counterbalanced by increases in defense, interest payments, and health care expenditures.

Ironically, the same conservative policymakers who increased the deficit in the 1980s now use it as an argument against more government spending. So much for fiscal responsibility.

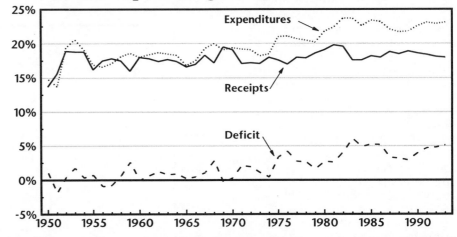

Federal budget receipts, expenditures, and deficit as a percentage of GDP, 1950-93

5.3 Government Spending Elsewhere

Knickerbocker

Americans who like to complain about Big Government might be surprised to discover that the governments of all major industrial nations, with the exception of Japan, spend more relative to their gross domestic product.

The Western European nations, particularly social democracies such as Austria and the Scandinavian countries, have a long tradition of high government spending. Germany, a major competitor of the U.S. in foreign trade, devotes about half its GDP to the public sector. So does Canada.

Patterns of spending are also different in the U.S., where military spending is relatively high. Even with lower overall levels of government spending, Japan devoted a larger share of its GDP to nonmilitary spending (about 19%) than did the U.S. in 1993.

Total government spending as a percentage of GDP, 1993
(includes federal, state, and local spending)

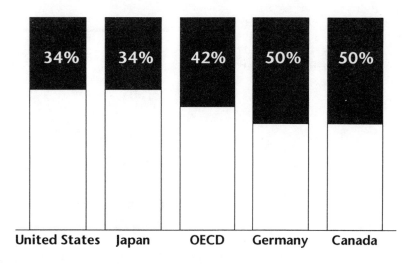

| United States | Japan | OECD | Germany | Canada |
| 34% | 34% | 42% | 50% | 50% |

5.4 Taxes Around the World

Knickerbocker

Nobody likes paying taxes. But U.S. workers pay lower income and payroll taxes, on average, than workers in other industrial countries (25% as compared with 33%).

Most businesses also pay higher taxes in other industrial countries. Japan and Germany have steeper corporate tax rates. In France and the U.K., employers make greater relative contributions to social security.

Although European workers pay more income and sales taxes, they enjoy a vast array of subsidized government services, including universal health care.

Comparative tax rates, 1991
(income and social security taxes as a percentage of income)

	Individual	Corporate
United States	25%	38%
Japan	16%	50%
Germany	38%	57%
OECD	33%	38%
Canada	22%	36%

5.5 Balanced Budget

Should the federal government make the reduction of the debt its number one objective? Proponents of balanced budgets say so. They argue that deficit reduction not only makes fiscal sense but would stimulate private investment by reducing interest rates.

But things are not so simple. The reduced spending and increased taxes needed to balance the budget would put a damper on the economy. Various studies of the impact of deficit reduction programs demonstrate that efforts to eliminate the deficit over a 4- or 5-year period could slow annual growth by half a percentage point and cost society 500,000 new jobs every year.

Also, the links between the size of the deficit, interest rates, and investment are weak. Corporate investment is influenced by the prospect of future sales, which could be darkened by slow growth. An alternative path to debt reduction would be to push the economy to grow faster than the debt.

5.6 Where Federal Dollars Go

How did Uncle Sam spend the "peace dividend"? Federal dollars are largely divided among the military, Social Security and Medicare, interest on the national debt, and human and physical resources. As a result of the war in Vietnam, military spending commanded 43% of the total budget in 1965. By 1995, the end of the Cold War had reduced this category to about 18% of the total.

Most of the savings were spent on increases in the share of Social Security and Medicare, which more than doubled between 1965 and 1995 (from 15% to 32%). An aging population, escalating medical costs, and benefits indexed against inflation all contributed to this trend.

Net interest payments, driven by large deficits and high interest rates, more than doubled their claims on the budget (from 7% to 14%).

Spending on other programs, primarily devoted to human and physical resources, now occupies about the same percentage of the federal budget as it did in 1965.

Components of the federal budget

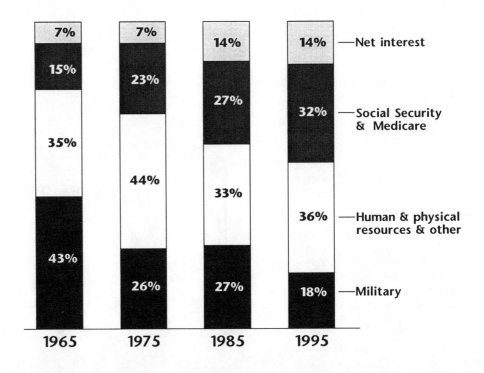

5.7 The Fate of Social Spending

Despite military cutbacks, spending on many social programs has declined as a percentage of all federal outlays. In 1994, Uncle Sam spent proportionately less on education, training, employment and social services, natural resources, the environment, and energy than in 1980.

Income security, a category that includes housing, food and nutrition assistance, unemployment compensation, and contributions to Aid to Families with Dependent Children, increased 0.6%. Reflecting trends elsewhere in the economy, the share of spending on health nearly doubled.

Social programs have proved susceptible to political attack, partly because of increased fiscal pressure. Higher mandatory expenditures such as interest on the national debt and payments for Social Security and Medicare, along with a reluctance to impose further cuts on the military, have put many social programs on the chopping block.

Selected social spending programs as a percentage of all federal outlays

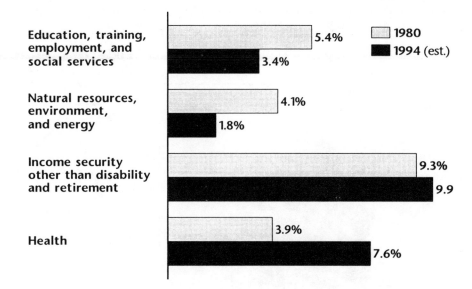

	1980	1994 (est.)
Education, training, employment, and social services	5.4%	3.4%
Natural resources, environment, and energy	4.1%	1.8%
Income security other than disability and retirement	9.3%	9.9
Health	3.9%	7.6%

5.8 Declining Public Investment

Falling bridges, gaping pot-holes, and poorly equipped schools are some of the most visible effects of budget cuts in the 1980s. Federal expenditures on infrastructure such as roads, airports, communications networks, civilian research and development, and education and training represent forms of investment that benefit the economy as a whole. Yet, from 1978 to 1994, expenditures in those areas declined from 14% to 9% of total federal spending.

Short-term budget cuts may well lead to long-term problems. The crumbling infrastructure hurts U.S. corporations as well as individual citizens. In 1993, the Clinton administration proposed spending $30 billion on a public investment package, but the idea was promptly nixed by a Congress more concerned with lowering the deficit.

OUR CRUMBLING INFRASTRUCTURE

Federal spending on infrastructure, civilian R&D, and education and training

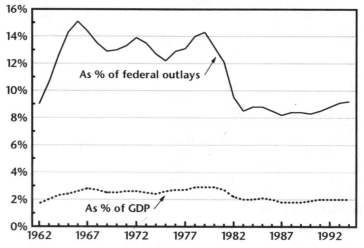

As % of federal outlays

As % of GDP

5.9 Policing the World

The U.S. might be keeping the world safe for capitalism, but at a high cost. Every year, about a quarter of federal spending, the equivalent of 5% of total GDP, goes to the armed forces. In 1992, the U.S. spent almost twice as much on its military as France, Germany, Japan, and the United Kingdom combined.

Are these expenditures necessary now that no "superpowers" pose any threat? The so-called archenemies of the U.S. are countries like Iran, Iraq, North Korea, and Syria. Even taken together, these countries have relatively little to spend on weapons and armies.

Cuts in military spending would not imperil national security. But they would threaten the industries and congressional districts that have come to depend on that spending.

Military expenditures, 1992
(billions of $1992)

281	U.S.
141	Germany, U.K., France, & Japan
47	Russia
22	Syria, Iran, Iraq, & N. Korea

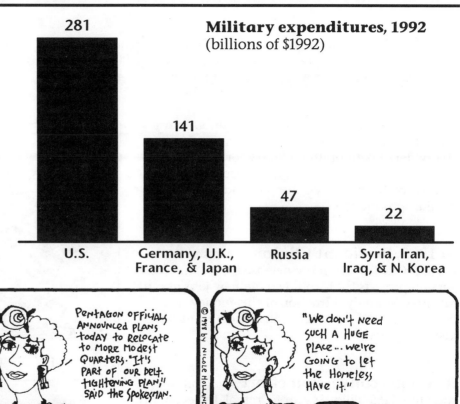

PENTAGON OFFICIALS ANNOUNCED PLANS TODAY TO RELOCATE TO MORE MODEST QUARTERS. "IT'S PART OF OUR BELT-TIGHTENING PLAN," SAID THE SPOKESMAN.

"WE DON'T NEED SUCH A HUGE PLACE... WE'RE GOING TO LET THE HOMELESS HAVE IT."

© 1988 by NICOLE HOLLANDER

5.10 Swords into Plowshares?

The Cold War is dead, but the military-industrial complex lives on, employing close to 6% of the labor force. More than 40,000 private firms with Pentagon contracts have been caught in a cycle of dependency.

Many industries, particularly shipbuilding, aircraft, and communication equipment, became overly dependent on the military for sales. Now they need to overcome the "gravy train" culture created by fat military contracts and convert to civilian production.

In 1992, President Clinton promised to move $60 billion from the defense budget into conversion projects that would create new jobs at old facilities. But only a fraction of this money has been spent, and no serious conversion plans have been proposed.

A serious conversion effort would entail spending $165 billion a year to "retool" the economy with better infrastructure, such as electric trains.

I KNOW, I KNOW... HE'S ROUGH ON MY ECONOMIC COMPETITIVENESS, ABUSIVE OF MY ENVIRONMENT... AND THIS NATIONAL SECURITY THING IS A JOKE, BUT I CAN'T IMAGINE LIFE WITHOUT HIM

MILITARY CODEPENDENCY COMPLEX

5.11 Where Taxes Come From

April 15 isn't the only day the federal government collects taxes. Social Security payments are deducted from most people's paychecks. Corporations are supposed to pay taxes on their profits. And the federal government collects sales taxes on some items, such as gasoline and cigarettes.

The relative importance of these sources of revenue has changed over time. Income taxes comprise about the same share today as they did in 1960, while taxes on corporate income have declined sharply, from 23% to 10% of the total. Sales taxes are also less important now than they once were.

Social Security has increased enormously in importance. It now accounts for 36% of the tax pie, relative to 16% in 1960. The payroll deduction was recently hiked, and a large generation of baby boomers is now paying into the system.

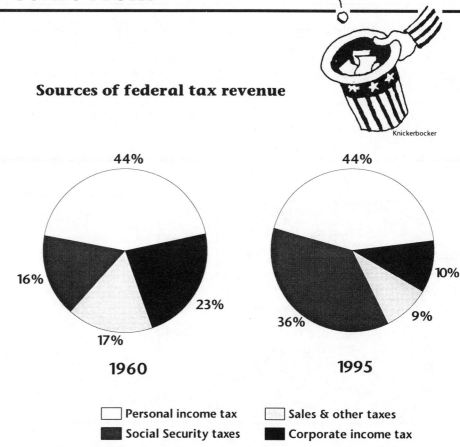

Sources of federal tax revenue

Knickerbocker

1960

44%

23%

17%

16%

1995

44%

10%

9%

36%

☐ **Personal income tax**   ☐ **Sales & other taxes**

■ **Social Security taxes**   ■ **Corporate income tax**

5.12 Corporate Taxes

From the hollers coming out of the business press, you might think that taxes are dragging the private sector down. But corporations rely on government spending not only for the enforcement of laws, development of infrastructure, and education of their workers but also for the provision of a stable economic environment. Corporations should pay their fair share.

Instead, they seem to be paying less and less. Back in the 1950s, federal taxes averaged about 45% of corporate profits. Today, they average only about 24%. New credits and generous depreciation allowances established in the early 1980s were intended to encourage investment. While they had little effect in that respect, they certainly made life easier for corporate executives and shareholders.

Corporate taxes as a percentage of profits, 1950-94

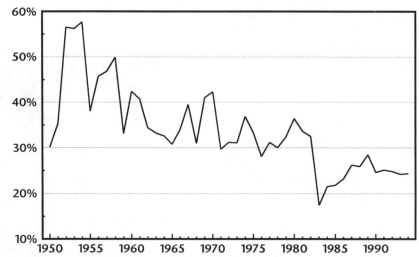

5.13 Who Got the Tax Break?

The rhetoric of tax relief helped the very rich. Between 1977 and 1992, tax rates on the top 1% of income earners declined dramatically, and almost everyone in the top 20% fared better. But the average tax rate did not change for the bottom 80% of the population, largely because increases in Social Security taxes counterbalanced slight declines in the income tax.

As a group, the top 1% saved $83 billion in 1992, compared with what they would have had to pay had 1977 tax rates remained in effect. This is more than the federal government spent on employment education, training, housing assistance, and social services in 1992.

Estimated effective federal tax rate for families

Income group	1977	1992
Bottom 80%	16.5%	16.5%
Top 20%	27.2%	26.8%
Top 1%	35.5%	29.3%

5.14 State and Local Taxes Are Regressive

In the name of the "New Federalism," Congress shifted responsibility for a number of social programs onto the states in the 1980s. As a result, the burden of taxation on low- and middle-income Americans was increased.

State and local governments rely heavily on regressive taxes (such as sales and property taxes) that take a bigger percentage out of low than out of high family incomes. The federal income tax, however, imposes higher rates on higher incomes. In 1993, 76% of all state and local tax revenue was raised by regressive taxes, compared with only 46% of federal revenue.

No wonder affluent voters like the idea of further decentralizing public spending—it will save them money. State-funded programs pit states against one another in efforts to attract industry with tax breaks and subsidies paid for by the poor and middle class.

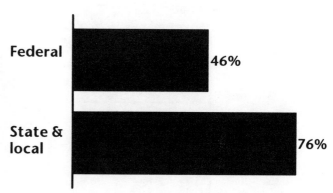

Percentage of tax revenue raised by regressive taxes, 1993

Federal 46%

State & local 76%

5.15 Corporate Subsidies

Peeved about the costs of Aid to Families with Dependent Children? Consider the costs of Aid to Dependent Corporations. Many different subsidies and tax breaks for corporations are tucked away in the federal budget, and they add up to a generous welfare program for the rich.

The savings and loan bailout has gotten some publicity, but its annual cost of about $18 billion is actually less than total subsidies to agriculture (including but not limited to price supports), which amounted to about $29 billion in 1992—more than was spent on Aid to Families with Dependent Children in the same year.

Uncle Sam has given even more support to the energy industry in the form of free services, subsidized insurance, and tax breaks for nuclear power, oil, and gas companies. The total price for citizens was about $35 billion in 1992—more than 35 times greater than the combined value of federal small business loans, support for mass transit, and spending on Head Start programs for children.

Corporate subsidies/tax breaks vs. other government subsidies, 1992
(billions of $1992)

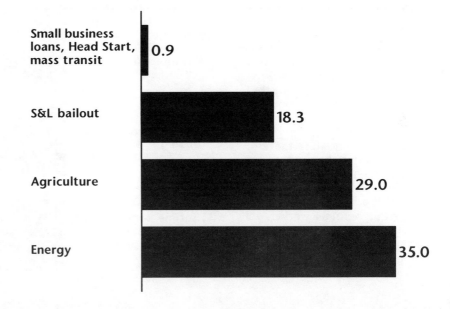

5.16 Social Security or Insecurity?

The Social Security system works a lot like a traditional family in which children support their parents in old age. The current working population is taxed to provide income and health care to the older generation. Payments made to retirees through Social Security and Medicare amount to more than twice the value of their contributions, plus interest, even for a single worker.

Yet some of these recipients already enjoy high incomes. Many did relatively little to help raise the generation of workers who are paying the Social Security bill. A single or divorced man with a history of high earnings gets more than a single or divorced mother who raised several children on her own but only intermittently worked for pay.

The system is also a bit precarious: Members of the "baby boom" generation worry that younger workers will have a hard time supporting them at the same level, especially since the relative size of the elderly population will be increasing.

Social Security tax contributions compared with Social Security and Medicare benefits (present value in $1990)

Total lifetime contributions (by employers and employees) plus interest — $83,852

Lifetime benefits for single worker — $184,082

Lifetime benefits for worker with non-employed spouse — $308,328

Chapter 6 **Education and Welfare**

Russell Christian

The fundamental test of an economy is its ability to meet human needs and give people a decent chance at happiness. The U.S. doesn't score as high on this test as it used to. Income inequality has intensified, poverty has spread, and homelessness has become a glaring problem in major cities. The economic importance of education has increased even as public commitment to support it has begun to decline.

Family incomes increased steadily between 1950 and the mid-1970s. Since then, only married couples with a wife in the paid labor force have managed to boost their median income. Women and mothers on their own remain economically disadvantaged (see *Chart 6.1*). Ever wonder why everyone you see in advertisements looks sleek and affluent? The very rich represent much of the country's buying power. As *Chart 6.2* shows, the top 5% of income earners has long received a larger share than the bottom 40%. In recent years, this inequality has intensified.

Poverty has grown deeper and meaner. *Chart 6.3* documents the recent increase in the numbers, even during a period of economic expansion. *Chart 6.4* shows which groups are most vulnerable to poverty—people of color and families raising children.

What does poverty really mean? No one is very happy with the standard definition. In some ways, it underestimates economic privation. In other ways, it overestimates it. These issues are outlined in *Chart 6.5*. Government programs benefit the elderly more than the young and have not done enough to enforce fathers' child support responsibilities. *Chart 6.6* points out that 22% of all children were growing up in poverty in 1992. What about the argument that poor people get too much assistance? As *Chart 6.7* shows, most government transfers go to the affluent, not to the needy. True, only the poor get "welfare."

Everybody else gets entitlements, subsidies, and tax breaks. Actually, less than half of the poor get any help at all from the federal government (*Chart 6.8*).

Those who have received cash assistance, primarily mothers raising children on their own, have seen the real value of their benefits decline substantially since 1970 (see *Chart 6.9*). It wouldn't cost that much to actually end poverty in this country. *Chart 6.10* offers some calculations.

The problems of the poor are often extreme versions of the problems everyone must face: finding a job, paying the rent, educating the kids, and staying healthy. As *Chart 6.11* shows, the costs of buying and renting have increased as a share of family income. This economic pinch helps explain why homelessness has become such a visible phenomenon. While estimates suggest that about half of the adult homeless also suffer from drug addiction or mental illness, many, including families with children, simply can't afford a place to live (*Chart 6.12*).

Education costs more than its used to. Average expenditures per pupil have been going up for some time (see *Chart 6.13*). But that doesn't mean that teachers and students are becoming less efficient. Education has become more demanding for a variety of reasons. Another problem is that educational expenditures are unequally distributed. Poor kids who attend poorly financed schools have a hard time getting good jobs and moving to better neighborhoods. *Chart 6.14* traces the effect of a political movement for school funding equalization, which is well under way in many states.

Recent initiatives to help college students have received a great deal of publicity. But they are too small-scale to help large numbers make their way through college. As *Chart 6.15* shows, higher education has become discouragingly expensive, especially at private schools. And federal aid to college students has declined. *Chart 6.16* offers evidence that students from low-income families may not be able to finish college, no matter how hard they study.

6.1 Family Income

Most families are on a treadmill, working harder and harder but barely maintaining their standard of living. Family incomes haven't increased much since the 1970s except for married couples with a wife in the paid labor force.

Worst-off are families maintained by women alone, many of which live in poverty. In recent years, the number of families in this category has increased, pulling average family income down.

Growing differences in family structure have contributed to increases in income inequality: Two-earner families without children can throw more money around than single mothers who are struggling to combine paid work with family responsibilities.

Some married women enter employment in order to compensate for stagnating family income. They often pay additional costs (such as daycare) that partially offset their earnings.

Median family income ($1992)

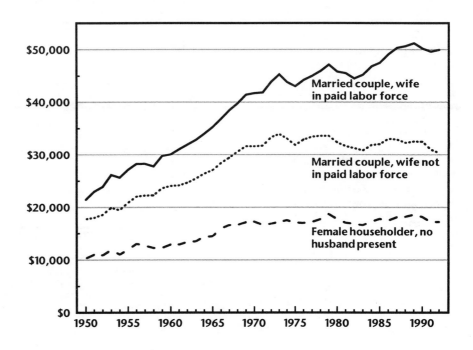

Married couple, wife in paid labor force

Married couple, wife not in paid labor force

Female householder, no husband present

6.2 Low-Income Households Get a Smaller Share

The rich keep on getting richer. Almost any way you measure it, the distribution of income worsened considerably in the 1980s, imposing new stresses on the social fabric. One of the most vivid indicators is the increased share of income enjoyed by the top 5% of all households.

Differences in buying power have always been immense, with the top 5% claiming a bigger hunk of all household income than the bottom 40%. But today's disparities are so great that even *Business Week* suggests that the growing gap between rich and poor may be hurting the economy.

The middle class is shrinking. Over the 1980s, the percentage of Americans earning more than 2 times median family income increased, as did the percentage earning half the median or less. (In 1992, the median family income for a family of 4 was about $40,000.)

Share of total household income received, by groups of households

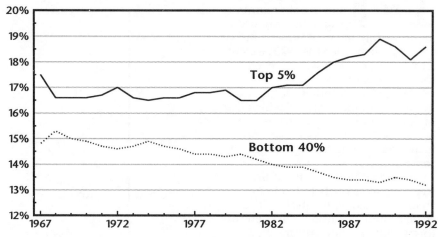

6.3 More Poor People

Poverty seems to be getting popular. The number of people with incomes under the poverty line tends to rise during recessions and fall during periods of economic growth. But underlying this wavy pattern is a definite upward trend since the late 1970s.

The number of poor diminished in the late 1960s and remained stable until about 1978. Then the War on Poverty began to turn into a War Against the Poor. High unemployment rates were accompanied by cuts in social spending. Real benefit levels provided by Aid to Families with Dependent Children (AFDC) fell. Politicians began blaming the poor for their own poverty and arguing that the benefits of growth would eventually trickle down to those willing to work.

But even during the economic expansion in the mid-1980s, the poor were largely left behind. Mink coats don't trickle down.

Millions of persons in poverty, 1967-92

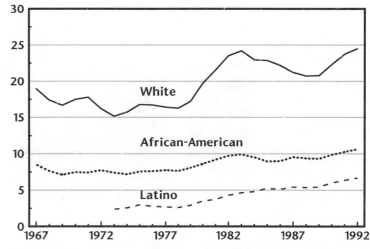

6.4 The Likelihood of Being Poor

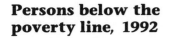overty threatens some far more than others. While the overall poverty rate for persons in 1992 was 15%, only 1 in 10 non-Latino whites was poor, compared with about 1 out of 3 African-Americans.

Whatever their race or background, families with children are more likely to live in poverty. Nearly half of all families with children under 18 maintained by women alone have incomes under the poverty line.

Canada, Australia, Sweden, Ger-many, the Netherlands, France, and Britain, unlike the U.S., all have government programs that provide a genuine safety net. The poverty rate for their children is about one-third that in the U.S.; for their elderly, the poverty rate is one-fourth as high.

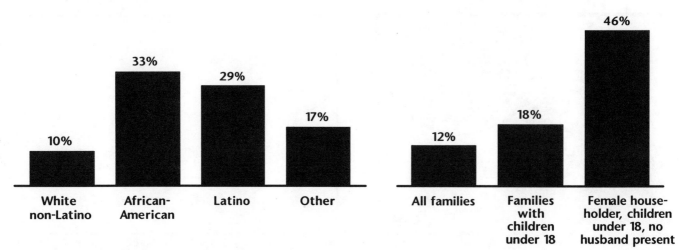

Persons below the poverty line, 1992

- White non-Latino: 10%
- African-American: 33%
- Latino: 29%
- Other: 17%

Families below the poverty line, 1992

- All families: 12%
- Families with children under 18: 18%
- Female house-holder, children under 18, no husband present: 46%

6.5 Defining Poverty

The poverty line, designated by the U.S. Census Bureau, varies according to family size and composition. In 1993, it was $14,764 for a 4-person family— less than 35% of the median income for married-couple families.

Defined in the 1960s as the amount of money required for a subsistence diet multiplied by 3, the poverty line has since been revised to account for changes in the cost of living.

Many experts argue that the poverty line is out-of-date because food costs are a smaller proportion of family budgets today. Another problem is that it fails to take into account the value of noncash transfers such as food stamps.

The poverty line also fails to take into account the costs of child care for working parents. A basic-needs budget for a mother who stays home with 2 children has been estimated at $10,847; for one who works outside the home it's about $24,262.

6.6 Poverty Among Children and the Elderly

Many of the elderly remain poor, but as a group they are better off than children, whose overall poverty rate increased from 17% in 1975 to 22% in 1992.

Many children are poor because they live in families that receive little or no financial support from an adult male. Government assistance is stingy. Unlike Social Security payments, real benefits provided by Aid to Families with Dependent Children have declined recently.

Even people unsympathetic to the poor tend to support Social Security, if only because they hope to receive it someday. But many people are not very concerned about other people's kids, particularly those of different racial or ethnic backgrounds.

And kids can't vote.

Percentage of children and elderly in poverty

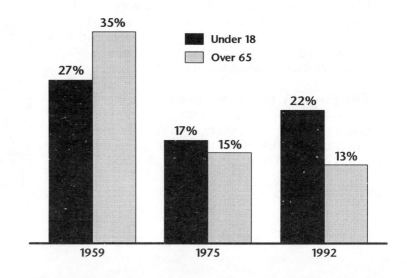

- **Under 18**
- **Over 65**

	1959	1975	1992
Under 18	27%	17%	22%
Over 65	35%	15%	13%

6.7 The Rich Get More Help Than the Poor

Federal transfers to the poor add up to less than the three largest tax breaks that benefit the middle class and wealthy: deductions for retirement plans, the deduction for home mortgage interest, and the exemption of health insurance premiums that companies pay for their employeees

Subsidies for mining, timber cutting, grazing, and irrigation cost the government over $200 million a year. Miners can take title to federal lands for as little as $2.50 an acre.

Adding together the value of direct benefits and tax breaks, an average household with income under $10,000 received roughly $5,700 from the government in 1991. The average household with an income over $100,000 collected $9,300.

6.8 Not All the Poor Get Help

The newspapers love to tell stories about welfare cheats. But they seldom report how many poor people are either ineligible or unwilling to receive public assistance. The government only recently began to collect survey data on program participation.

These data show that in 1992, only 43% of poor people collected cash assistance and only slightly more than half benefited from food stamps or Medicaid.

Critics often speak of welfare as though it were an addictive drug with permanent side effects. One of the few studies of families over a 10-year period, however, shows that Aid to Families with Dependent Children (AFDC) helped many regain their economic health. The overwhelming majority received cash assistance for less than 2 years.

Percentage of poor persons in households participating in federal poverty programs, 1992

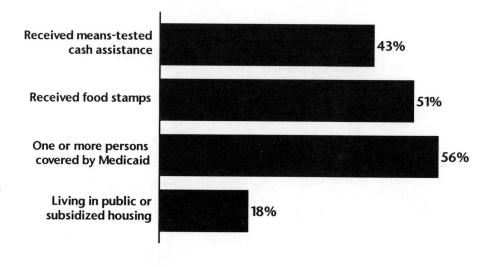

Received means-tested cash assistance	43%
Received food stamps	51%
One or more persons covered by Medicaid	56%
Living in public or subsidized housing	18%

6.9 Less Public Assistance

Poor women and children have never received very generous assistance from Aid to Families with Dependent Children (AFDC). But since 1970, real benefits have declined.

In 1970, benefits averaged about $622 per family per month (measured in constant $1992), or about 71% of the poverty line for a family of 3. By 1992, they had fallen to $374, or about 40% of the poverty line.

In contrast, the families of widows or widowers eligible for survivor's benefits through Social Security could expect cash benefits of about 3 times as much, with no wealth restrictions or work requirements.

The 50 states offer widely varying maximum AFDC payments, ranging in 1990 from $115 a month in Alabama to $637 a month in California.

Average monthly AFDC payments per family ($1992)

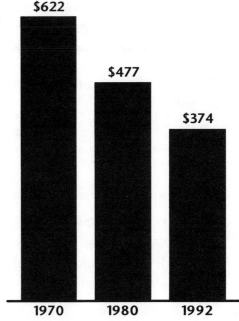

1970	1980	1992
$622	$477	$374

THE MEDIA CALL IT "COMPASSION FATIGUE" -- THE GROWING SENSE IN OUR SOCIETY THAT, AFTER A DECADE OF *IGNORING* THE HOMELESS, IT IS NOW TIME TO ACTIVELY *PERSECUTE* THEM...

I USED TO FEEL KIND OF *SORRY* FOR THOSE PEOPLE--

..BUT THEY'RE ALL SO *ICKY!* I WISH THEY'D JUST GO AWAY!

THIS "BLAME-THE-VICTIM" MENTALITY IS ENCOURAGED BY IDEOLOGUES WHO INSIST THAT THE HOMELESS SIMPLY *DON'T WANT TO WORK*...

THAT'S RIGHT! THEY HAVE *CHOSEN* LIVES OF HUNGER, DISCOMFORT, FILTH, PAIN, DISEASE AND DEGRADATION--

--BECAUSE THEY ARE *LAZY!*

mail: TOM.TOMORROW@SFNET.COM

6.10 The Cost of Ending Poverty

In 1992, *Business Week* estimated that poverty-related crime in the U.S. cost the country $50 billion and that productive employment for the poor could generate $60 billion. In that year, additional public transfers of $45.8 billion could have brought the incomes of all families over the poverty line.

That $45.8 billion represented:

- 💰 less than 1% of gross domestic product
- 💰 about 15% of military spending

Poverty among children could have been eliminated by transfers of little more than half that amount—$28 billion. According to the Congressional Budget Office, the U.S. could easily have raised that amount of money simply by taxing the richest 1% of Americans at the same rates in effect in 1977.

Poverty could be ended even more cheaply if:

- 💰 The unemployment rate were lowered to 4%.
- 💰 The minimum wage were raised to $5.25 an hour.
- 💰 All citizens enjoyed health insurance.
- 💰 Publicly subsidized high-quality daycare were increased and school schedules were modifed to accomodate working parents.

TOLES copyright The Buffalo News. Reprinted with permission of Universal Press Syndicate. All rights reserved.

6.11 Higher Housing Costs

Home is where the heart is—and where most of the money goes. Between 1979 and 1991, housing costs increased dramatically, and family income failed to keep pace. As a result, fewer people were able to buy homes, and those who did often found themselves mired in debt.

By 1991, the average homeowner with a mortgage spent 25% of family income making payments, compared with 21% in 1979. Many low-income families have a hard time renting, much less buying, decent housing. In 1991, they spent an average of 15% of their income on rent.

Most families still enjoy a substantial federal subsidy for home ownership—they can deduct their interest payments from their taxable income. But federal assistance for low-income families has declined.

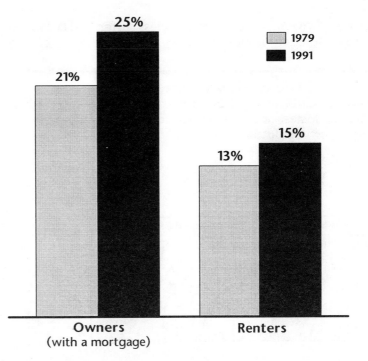

Monthly costs of a home as a percentage of family income

- 1979
- 1991

Owners (with a mortgage): 21% (1979), 25% (1991)
Renters: 13% (1979), 15% (1991)

6.12 Homeless in America

Up to 7 million people were homeless at some point in the late 1980s. Current estimates range from 500,000 to several million.

An estimated 50% of the adult homeless suffer from drug addiction or mental illness.

In 1991, 34% of the nation's homeless were families with children (up from 27% in 1985). They are the fastest-growing segment of America's homeless population.

During the 1980s, the federal government reduced appropriations for low-income housing by 81%, adjusting for inflation.

In fiscal 1992, total state appropriations for emergency housing programs for the homeless were cut 10%, adjusting for inflation.

THERE SEEM TO BE MORE AND MORE PEOPLE SLEEPING IN THE STREETS

SOME OF THEM ARE MENTALLY ILL, JUNKIES AND DRUNKS

WHAT ABOUT THE OTHERS?

NOBODY CAN FIGURE IT OUT

RENTS SOAR WAGES FALL

6.13 Education Costs More

Education doesn't come cheap. Even controlling for inflation, average expenditures per pupil in U.S. schools have increased steadily since 1970. New legal requirements have set high standards for the special education of handicapped and disabled students. The number of students who are not native English speakers has increased.

Many social trends make teachers' work more difficult. Because more parents are working long hours to earn enough money to support their families, they have less time to help children with homework. Studies show that kids who spend hours in front of a television don't develop good reading skills.

Yet children today need to learn even more than their parents did. A high-tech economy requires high-tech schools and high-quality teachers.

Average expenditures per pupil in public elementary and secondary schools ($1992)

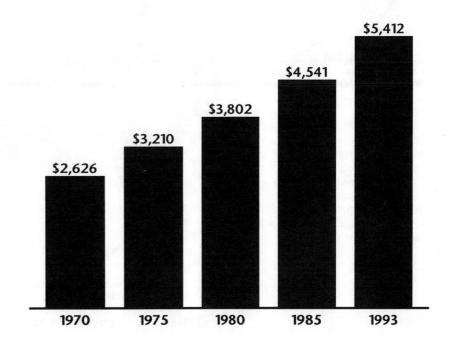

1970	1975	1980	1985	1993
$2,626	$3,210	$3,802	$4,541	$5,412

6.14 Poor Schools for Poor Kids

Most public schools in the U.S. rely heavily on local property taxes, leading to considerable inequality in funding. In some states, affluent school districts spend 9 times as much per pupil as poorer districts.

Recent studies suggest that greater per-pupil expenditures on classroom instruction raise test scores and future earnings.

While the U.S. Constitution makes few references to education, many state constitutions promise educational opportunity to all citizens. As of June 1993, lawsuits were challenging school funding systems in more than a third of the states, and courts in at least 13 states had found school funding systems to be unconstitutional.

Challenges to school finance systems

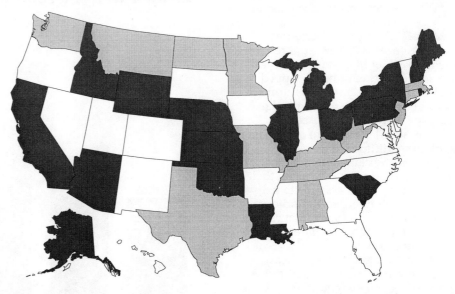

☐ **States in which school finance system has been found unconstitutional by state courts**

■ **States in which school finance system is currently being challenged**

6.15 The Rising Cost of College

Knickerbocker

The price of admission is being marked up at both private and public universities. A hundred grand is no longer enough to buy 4 years at Yale. On average, the costs of private universities now exceed 50% of median family income, putting them well beyond the reach of most families.

Public universities charge less, ranging from $11,726 a year for in-state students at the University of Vermont to $5,504 at the University of North Carolina. But as state legislatures cut back on state support, public universities and colleges must raise tuition and fees. Students and their families now pay costs once shouldered by taxpayers.

Why have private schools hiked tuition? Many of their costs, including health insurance, have increased. Also, many have invested in new computers and other equipment. Faculty salaries have increased hardly at all in recent years. The number of highly paid administrators, however, has grown quite rapidly.

University tuition, room, and board costs as a percentage of median family income

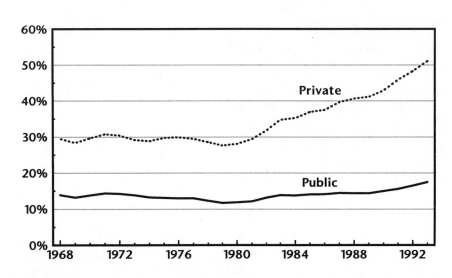

6.16 Public Aid to College Students

Knickerbocker

With tuition on the rise, college students have become increasingly dependent on outside help. But public aid has declined as a percentage of per capita income. Most recent innovations, such as AmeriCorps, the national service program, make it easier for students to borrow money but don't help the truly needy. The average level of outright assistance has plummeted.

As one policy analyst explains, "We're headed toward a price-based admission policy where the people who can afford it will go to college and the others won't." In 1979, a student from the richest income quartile was 4 times more likely to earn a B.A. by age 24 than a student in the poorest quartile. By 1994, that individual was 19 times more likely. So much for equal opportunity.

Public spending per higher education student as a percentage of U.S. income per capita

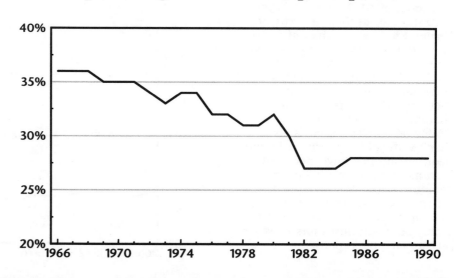

Chapter 7 **Health**

Russell Christian

The U.S. health care system is clearly in pain, but the politicians in charge spend most of their time bickering with one another. Take a look at the country's medical history. As *Chart 7.1* reveals, U.S. expenditures have increased steadily as a percentage of GDP and are far higher than those of other industrialized countries. Much of this increased spending reflects waste and inefficiency.

The health care sector is unique. People don't go shopping for medical services the way they do for groceries or a car: They rely on medical providers to tell them what they need and are seldom in a position to quibble over prices. Most bills are paid either through insurance or by the government. And as *Chart 7.2* shows, government and businesses combined account for most health spending.

The prices of health-related goods and services, pictured in *Chart 7.3*, have risen much more rapidly than the Consumer Price Index. The following charts explore these price increases in more detail and suggest that they are related to problems in the organization of the health care industry. Declining hospital use has actually contributed to higher costs for a hospital stay. Competing for more customers, hospitals engage in a technological "arms race," acquiring more and more sophisticated equipment (*Chart 7.4*). Pharmaceutical companies charge extremely high prices and enjoy extremely large profits (*Chart 7.5*). Physicians can make so much money in highly paid specialties that many are reluctant to enter general practice (*Chart 7.6*).

Last, but not least, Americans have to pay extra for the privilege of choosing among more than 1,200 insurance companies, all of which use slightly different forms with slightly different rules. The paperwork is overwhelming and adds up to high administrative costs. *Chart 7.7* points out that government-run systems spend far less on overhead.

So much money, such poor health. Despite high expenditures, the U.S. is ranked extremely low on overall measures such as life expectancy and infant mortality (*Chart 7.8*). The most obvious reason is the extraordinary inequality of health care in this country. Of all the industrialized countries, only the U.S. fails to provide health benefits for all its citizens.

The comfortable classes not only have better access to doctors and hospitals; they also live in healthier neighborhoods and work in healthier jobs (*Chart 7.9*). As *Chart 7.10* shows, the rising cost of health care means that poor people must spend a very large percentage of their income to obtain it.

Racial and ethnic inequalities are conspicuous. In many neighborhoods of this country, children of color have a smaller chance of surviving to adulthood than in the least developed nations of the world. Partly because of poor delivery of prenatal care, the ratio of black infant deaths per 1,000 to white infant deaths per 1,000 increased significantly in the 1980s (*Chart 7.11*).

Many people of color lack health insurance: more than 1 out of every 3 Latinos and 1 out of every 5 African-Americans (*Chart 7.12*). Class inequalities are equally significant. *Chart 7.13* shows that many people simply don't have the money to buy health insurance.

Nor do they have the money to lobby for change. In 1993 and 1994, special-interest groups spent more than $100 million to influence health care reform legislation, scrambling to protect their own pocketbooks. One of the best reform alternatives, a single-payer system, was ignored by most lobbyists, as well as the media. *Chart 7.14* outlines some of the good features of this system, which serves Canadians well.

However pressing the need for reform in the U.S., it is important to maintain an international perspective. Many developing countries suffer from diseases that they have the know-how but not the money to control (*Chart 7.15*). And the spread of HIV and AIDS is one of most acute public health problems in the world. Research, prevention, and treatment efforts are even more inadequate in the developing world than in this country. *Chart 7.16* emphasizes the need for global mobilization against AIDS.

7.1 The Unhealthy Cost of Health Care

Excess and deprivation describe the paradox of health care in the U.S. We spend a much larger share of our gross domestic product (GDP) on health than other advanced industrialized nations, even though 40 million of our citizens—1 person in 6—lack health insurance.

Furthermore, our health costs have increased more sharply since the 1970s than those in other countries, largely because we have failed to develop a comprehensive, well-coordinated health care delivery system. Instead, we rely on a patchwork of private insurance and public assistance that finances luxury treatment for some but begrudges even emergency treatment to others (with a huge amount of paperwork for all).

Doctors and hospitals are torn between the demands of profit maximization and the principles of respect for human life. And even patients with insurance wonder what will happen when it runs out.

Health spending as a percentage of GDP

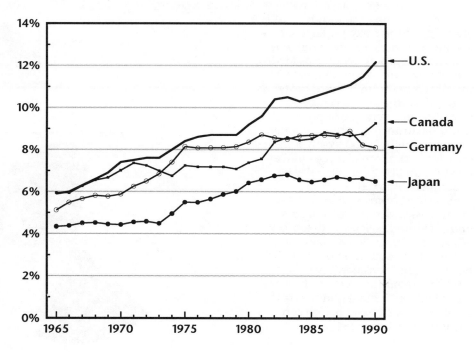

7.2 Who Pays for Health Care?

Very few people actually buy their health care over the counter. Many have employer-provided insurance that is considered part of their pay package. Others buy insurance or are covered by government programs such as Medicare. As a result, payment for services usually comes from a "third party" rather than the actual consumer.

Many employers like to provide health insurance because it is a nontaxable benefit: $1,000 worth of insurance is worth more to a potential employee than $1,000 in extra pay because it is not taxed.

As insurance costs go up, however, many businesses are cutting back and providing policies with less coverage and higher deductibles. The share of the population over age 65 has increased considerably since 1965. The mounting cost of Medicare and Medicaid helps explain why the government's share of health care spending has increased.

Components of health care spending, 1991

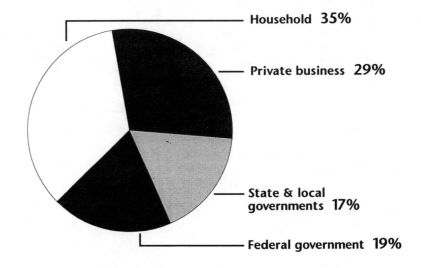

Household **35%**

Private business **29%**

State & local governments **17%**

Federal government **19%**

7.3 High Cost Fever

Any doctor examining this chart should be able to tell that the patient in question, health care, is very sick. While consumer prices increased by more than 3½ times between 1970 and 1993, medical costs grew by a factor of more than 6. The upward trend finally slowed in 1994, but not by much.

Rising costs are partly due to the rapid pace of technological change in medicine. But the fact that other countries have kept medical costs under control suggests that the structure of our health care system is a problem.

Better insurance coverage, however important, won't keep costs under control. We need to diagnose—and cure—some diseases that seem to afflict hospitals, the pharmaceutical industry, physicians, and insurance companies.

Price indices for medical costs
(1970 = 100)

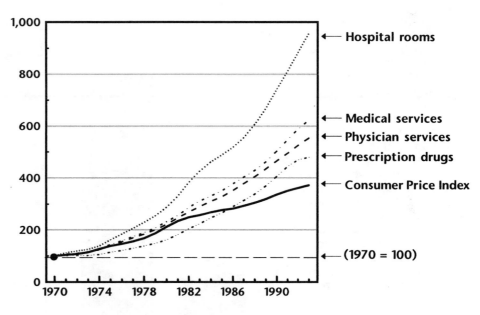

← Hospital rooms

← Medical services
← Physician services
← Prescription drugs

← Consumer Price Index

← (1970 = 100)

7.4 A Day in the Hospital

Hospitals cost so much now that doctors prescribe them less. Widespread efforts to limit admissions and shorten the average length of stay have been successful. But costs keep going up, as hospitals vie for doctors who can attract well-insured customers.

Competition keeps prices down, right? Not in this case. Studies show that the cost per admission is 25% higher in hospitals facing substantial local competition.

Here's why: Hospitals attract doctors and their patients, not by advertising the cheapest rates in town, but by offering the highest-quality care. Because this is often equated with availability of the latest high-tech equipment, hospitals often get caught up in a medical "arms race" that leads them to buy more than they can efficiently utilize.

Average daily cost of a hospital stay
($1992)

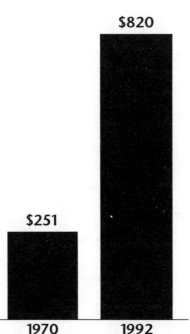

$251 — 1970

$820 — 1992

Nicole Hollander

7.5 Rx = Big Bucks

For the past 30 years, says *Fortune* magazine, drug makers have "enjoyed the fattest profits in big business....No American industry has ever defied the laws of economic gravity like pharmaceuticals."

How did they do it? Largely by raising prices. Since 1970, prescription drug prices have risen much faster than the overall rate of inflation. Companies argue that the money is needed to develop new drugs. But the industry as a whole typically spends $1 billion more annually on advertising than on research. Moreover, a large percentage of new products are actually "me-too" drugs that make no new contribution to existing therapies.

In Canada and the United Kingdom, countries with a single-payer health system, the government negotiates prices directly with pharmaceutical companies. As a result, many of the same drugs cost only half as much.

Russell Christian

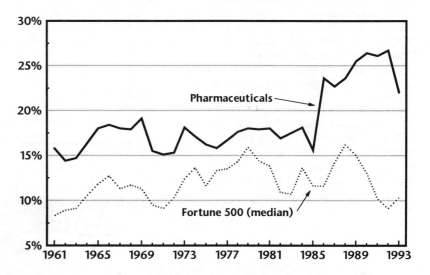

Return on stockholders' equity, 1961-93

Pharmaceuticals

Fortune 500 (median)

7.6 It Pays to Specialize

Doctors rightfully complain about the rising costs of paperwork and malpractice insurance. But even taking these costs into account, specialists in surgery, radiology, and obstetrics have enjoyed significant increases in their net income. General practitioners have seen their net income decline a bit, but they still earn more than 4 times as much as ordinary people.

Doctors in general earn far more in this country than they do elsewhere: twice as much as in Germany and Canada and 3 times as much as in Japan and Great Britain. Yet there are no fewer doctors per capita in those countries.

There are fewer specialists. In Canada, for instance, 90% of doctors provide primary care. In many countries, government agencies regulate the placement of medical students in specialty training and negotiate with doctors to keep a lid on fees.

Physicians' median net income compared with median earnings of all full-time wage and salary workers (thousands of $1992)

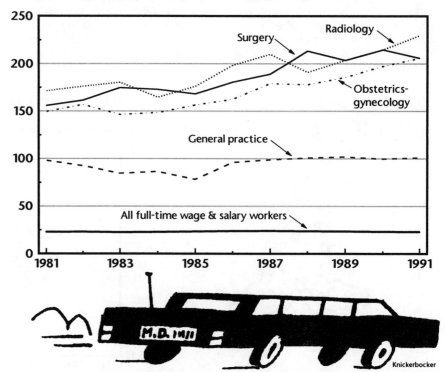

Knickerbocker

7.7 Insurance Overhead

Contrary to popular belief, more government could mean *less* bureaucracy. At least $45 billion was spent administering the American health care system in 1992. A huge amount of money could be saved by switching to a single-payer system.

Private insurance companies have higher administrative overhead than public programs like Medicaid and Medicare. They spend money to advertise and sell their products, and they must charge extra to make a profit. This overhead amounts to about 14 cents of every dollar actually spent.

In the Canadian public single-payer system, overhead accounted for only about 1% of total program expenditures in 1987. Doctors and hospitals there do far less paperwork because they don't have to deal with scores of different insurance companies.

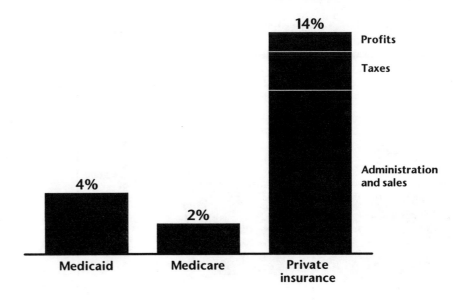

Administrative overhead as percentage of total program expenditures, 1992

14%

Profits

Taxes

Administration and sales

4%

2%

Medicaid **Medicare** **Private insurance**

7.8 Spend More, Live Less

Americans just don't live as long, on average, as citizens of other industrialized countries, even though we spend more per capita on health services than anyone else.

Twenty-three other countries have infant mortality rates lower than ours. Why? Other countries provide health services on the basis of need, but the U.S. allocates services by patients' ability to pay. Citizens of other industrial countries see physicians more often and enjoy longer hospital stays. They also pay less for those services than we do.

The U.S. has higher poverty rates, and poverty itself is bad for health. Also, more people in the U.S. die crime-related deaths, particularly in poor neighborhoods.

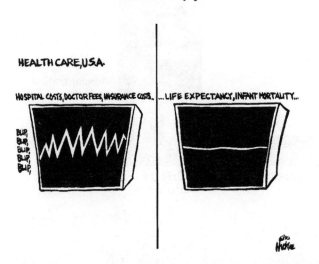

HEALTH CARE, U.S.A.

HOSPITAL COSTS, DOCTOR FEES, INSURANCE COSTS.

...LIFE EXPECTANCY, INFANT MORTALITY...

BLIP
BLIP
BLIP
BLIP
BLIP

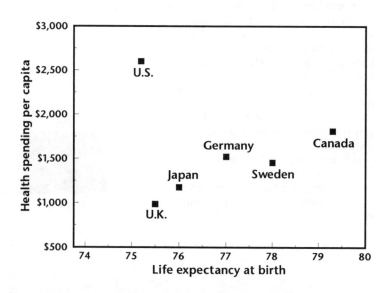

Life expectancy and health spending, 1990

7.9 Rich People Feel Better

oney is good for your health (and vice versa). Over 50% of the affluent individuals in the top income group consider themselves in excellent health, but only 26% of those in the bottom group say the same. Not surprisingly, many more poor people than rich people describe their health as poor.

High income provides easier access to health care and usually improves the conditions under which people live and work. Unsafe neighborhoods and poor working conditions are major health problems for low-income families. Also, those without health insurance often postpone or fail to get medical treatment, which can aggravate their condition.

Some people get caught in a health-poverty trap: Poor health makes it difficult for them to find and keep a well-paying job. And without that job, they can't get the health care they need.

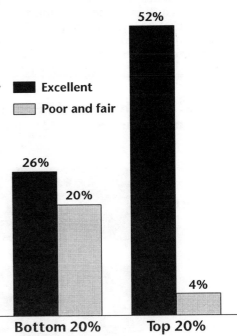

Self-assessed health status, by income group, 1991

- ■ Excellent
- ▨ Poor and fair

52%
26% 20%
4%

Bottom 20%   Top 20%

Tom Tomorrow

7.10 Poor People Pay More

No wonder most affluent families don't worry about health care. The richest fifth spend only about 15% of their income on health insurance premiums, out-of-pocket payments, and taxes devoted to health care. In return, they generally enjoy excellent services. The poorest fifth, on the other hand, spend 23% of their family income on health care, and lack of insurance coverage sometimes means long waits in hospital emergency rooms. For them, a trip to the hospital can mean no money for next month's rent.

Doctors, medicine, and insurance cost about the same whether you are rich or poor. If more health care were financed through taxation, rather than private insurance, the burden could be more equally distributed.

Also, the risks could be more evenly spread. Many middle-class workers who currently have health insurance may lose it if they get laid off. And insurance companies sometimes refuse to enroll individuals with "pre-existing medical conditions."

Total health expenditures as percentage of family income, 1992

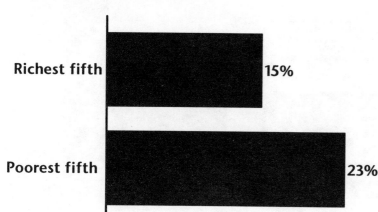

Richest fifth — 15%

Poorest fifth — 23%

7.11 Black Children at Greater Risk

Nothing symbolizes the inadequacies of the U.S. health care system more vividly than disparities in the mortality rates of children of different races.

In 1991, the black infant mortality rate was 16.5 for every 1,000 live births, compared with 7.5 for whites. Overall, black infants in the U.S. are worse off than those in such nations as Jamaica, Trinidad and Tobago, and Chile. Some inner-city neighborhoods have infant mortality rates as high as 30 per 1,000.

Poor prenatal care, related to lack of health insurance coverage, accounts for much of the problem. The increasing ratio of black to white infant deaths also reflects the general increase in income inequality and poverty.

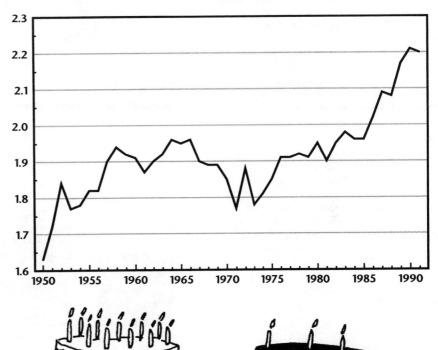

Ratio of black infant deaths per 1,000 to white infant deaths per 1,000

Knickerbocker

7.12 People of Color Lack Health Insurance

Knickerbocker

Most diseases don't discriminate, and accidents can happen to anyone, regardless of the color of their skin. But access to health care, like poverty and unemployment, reflects racial and ethnic inequalities. More than a fifth of all African-Americans and 38% of all Mexican-Americans lacked health insurance in 1992, compared with 18% of Puerto Ricans and 16% of whites.

Important regional and historical factors help explain why Mexican-Americans are particularly vulnerable. Most live in southwestern states where jobs offer fewer benefits and public assistance is slim. Also, many are immigrants concentrated in low-paying jobs. Some are unfamiliar with the U.S. health care system, and a few are illegal immigrants who are afraid to seek medical assistance because of the threat of deportation.

Percentage of people under 65 in various racial and ethnic groups lacking health insurance, 1992

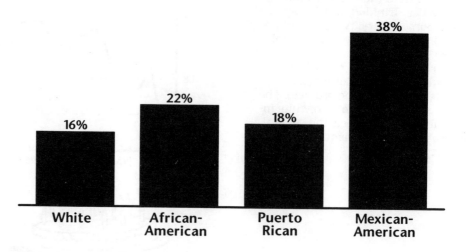

7.13 Poor Coverage for the Poor

When poor people get sick, they often have no choice but to go to a hospital emergency room and beg for help. While the federal Medicare system covers people age 65 and over, Medicaid provides assistance for only about half of the poor.

In 1992, about 36% of all people under 65 with incomes under $14,000 lacked health insurance, mostly because they couldn't afford it. The overall percentage for Americans under 65 was about 17%.

Most of the uninsured fell into the category of the working poor: 85% lived in households headed by a worker and would therefore benefit from employer benefits if they were provided.

Insurance coverage varies by region. In some areas of the South and West, where Medicaid is less generous and workers are less unionized, 25% of the population lacks health insurance.

Percentage of people under 65 lacking health insurance, by income group, 1992

- More than $50,000 — 4%
- $35,000 to $49,999 — 7%
- $25,000 to $34,999 — 14%
- $14,000 to $24,999 — 28%
- Less than $14,000 — 36%

The Canadian "single-payer" health care system provides universal coverage with high quality at a low cost.

Cost Control. Planning, rather than competition, keeps costs down. Hospitals and clinics have set budgets; doctors' fees and pharmaceutical prices are negotiated. Paperwork is simplified and streamlined.

Access and Fairness. No "tiers" or "classes" of coverage based on income. Health care is financed through taxes, rather than insurance payments.

Quality. Critics of the single-payer approach claim that it offers less choice, lower quality, and long waiting lines. But under the Canadian system, patients get the physicians of their choice. And while some medical procedures are not readily available, studies show that the Canadian system delivers more high-tech procedures to more people than the current U.S. system. In 1990, over 50% of Canadians expressed satisfaction with their health care system, compared with only 10% of U.S. citizens.

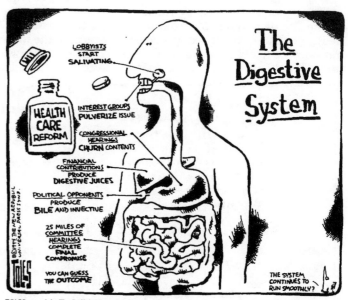

7.15 Global Health

Knickerbocker

Health problems that have been eliminated in affluent countries still ravage developing nations, where infectious and parasitic diseases account for 50% of all deaths (compared with 1% in developed countries). More than three-quarters of these deaths occur among children under 5 years of age.

Progress has been made in child immunization, but tropical diseases such as malaria and schistosomiasis are making a comeback, as mosquitoes and parasites develop resistance to commonly used pesticides and drugs.

A billion people in less developed countries lack access to safe drinking water. Far more die from diarrhea than from cancer. Air pollution is a growing problem not only in big cities but also in rural areas where people rely on wood and dung fires.

Economic underdevelopment kills people.

Health conditions, and mortality rates for children under 5, 1990

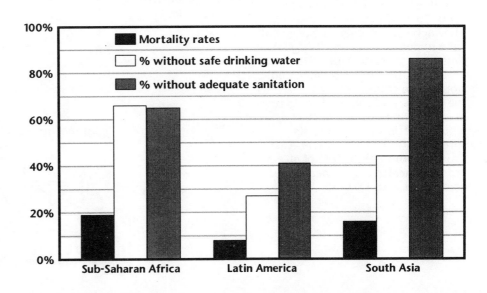

Legend:
- ■ Mortality rates
- □ % without safe drinking water
- ▨ % without adequate sanitation

Categories: Sub-Saharan Africa, Latin America, South Asia

7.16 AIDS Around the World

A horrible disease is spreading at an alarming rate. Today, more than 1 million people have AIDS, and 13 million HIV-positive individuals can expect to suffer and die from it.

The overwhelming majority of HIV infections are found in developing countries, with more than half in Africa alone. These are countries that cannot afford to treat the disease: They account for only 10% of global AIDS expenditures even though they must care for 82% of all AIDS victims.

In sub-Saharan Africa, men and women are equally likely to contract the disease, and many children have been orphaned by it. Health care systems are crumbling under the pressure. In Uganda, for example, AIDS consumes more than 50% of all government health care expenditures (compared with 1% in the U.S.).

Distribution of AIDS and AIDS spending
(as of January 1, 1992)

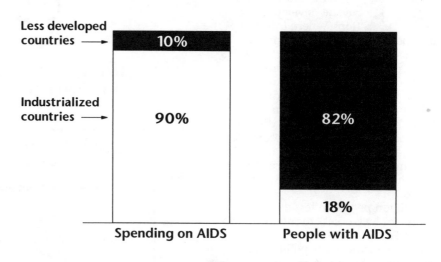

Less developed countries →

Industrialized countries →

Spending on AIDS	People with AIDS
10%	82%
90%	18%

Knickerbocker

Chapter 8 **Environment**

Russell Christian

From emission controls to containment vessels, from silent spring to nuclear winter, environmental hazards have created a vivid new vocabulary of concern. Conservatives repeat an old refrain: Don't interfere with the marketplace. But the energy sources we now rely on have dangerous side effects that are not reflected in their prices. And many of the "goods" that are most precious to us—good air, good water, and good health—don't have a price tag on them at all.

Environmentalists are often suspicious of emphasis on economic growth, and with good reason. Economists typically define growth in ways that have little to do with people's welfare and are probably unsustainable. *Chart 8.1* contrasts the growth of per capita GNP with a measure of Sustainable Eco-

nomic Welfare, which has actually declined since the 1960s. *Chart 8.2* summarizes some information about the most global of environmental threats, the deterioration of the ozone layer.

Other global problems that result from unregulated growth include the loss of land due to overgrazing, deforestation, agricultural mismanagement, and pollution *(Chart 8.3)* and the increased rate of extinction of many animal and plant species (*Chart 8.4).*

Trash is getting harder to dispose of. In many areas of the country, mapped in *Chart 8.5,* improperly stored hazardous materials pose a major public health threat. Communities don't want to devote precious space to more and more landfills. As *Chart 8.6* shows, recycling is increasing, but not enough to make up for increased quantities of solid wastes.

Despite the environmentalist legislation of the 1970s, pollution continues to despoil our water and air. The "easy" part has already been accomplished. Tough new strategies are needed to deal with decentralized problems such as fertilizer runoff and acid rain. As *Chart 8.7* shows, bacteria counts in rivers and streams have actually increased in recent years. While new smokestack restrictions have reduced the amount of particles in the air since 1950, emissions of sulfur and nitrogen dioxides are up (see *Chart 8.8*).

Part of the problem lies in the profligate way our economy uses energy. Apart from the fact that we consume a far greater share of fossil fuels than our share of the world population warrants (see *Chart 8.9*), almost all forms of energy consumption have a bad effect on the environment. The market price of most forms of energy remains far below the true price (which should take into account environmental impacts). *Chart 8.10* presents some estimates of the true cost of several important energy sources.

Whatever the limits of markets, they still have an important role to play. Often, government actions, including state planning, wreak just as much environmental havoc as big business. *Chart 8.11* outlines this issue and points out that at least some environmentalists support market-based strategies, such as tradable "pollution permits."

One reason for strong international regulation, however, is that big mistakes generate big bills. *Chart 8.12* documents the enormous environmental costs of man-made disasters such as the *Exxon Valdez* oil spill, the Chernobyl meltdown, and the Persian Gulf War.

What about the economics of regulation within the U.S.? The Environmental Protection Agency plays a crucial but limited role. The agency lacks the political support and funds it needs to develop a truly comprehensive environmental defense system, and as *Chart 8.13* shows, its small share of the total federal budget has declined in recent years. On the bright side, the private sector has begun to pay more attention to pollution control and is spending more money and creating more jobs in this area than it used to (see *Chart 8.14*).

It is important to remember that many environmental problems have an uneven influence. Rich people can buy property in unspoiled sylvan areas and travel to unpolluted beaches. Poor people can't. In this country, race also has a discernible impact. As *Chart 8.15* points out, people of color are more likely to live in communities with air pollution, toxic waste, and other hazards.

International differences are also significant. While many policymakers complain about rapid population growth in developing countries, citizens of the developed countries consume far more resources and generate far more waste and pollution per capita. As *Chart 8.16* shows, some economists have actually promoted the growing trend toward the "export" of waste to poor countries.

8.1 GNP Is Misleading

Are things getting better or worse? Economists like to measure our collective well-being by counting up the value of everything that is bought and sold and dividing it by the size of the population—gross national product (GNP) per capita. But even they admit that this is a misleading indicator because it doesn't include the value of things that don't carry an explicit price tag, such as breathable air, swimmable rivers, and livable neighborhoods.

When the *Exxon Valdez* spilled tons of crude oil into Alaskan waters in 1989, the money spent trying to clean up actually increased GNP, even though it was inadequate to compensate for damage to the environment.

An alternative index of "sustainable economic welfare" (SEW) gives a better picture of the quality of life. It includes the value of purchased items but adds estimates of the value of nonmarket services (such as time devoted to housework and childcare) and subtracts the costs of pollution, resource depletion, and long-term environmental damage. It also takes inequality of income into account.

This measure gives a very different picture of recent trends. GNP per capita has increased considerably, despite occasional dips. But SEW was lower in 1990 than in 1966.

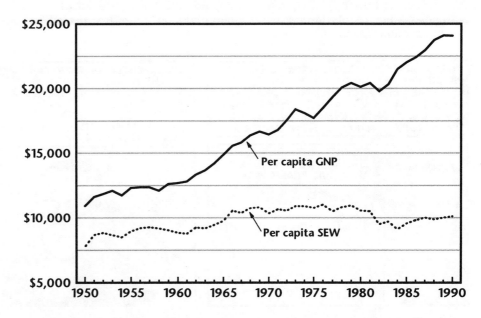

Measures of economic welfare in the U.S.
($1992)

Per capita GNP

Per capita SEW

8.2 Bye-Bye Ozone

The ozone layer, 12 to 30 miles above the earth, absorbs about 99% of the sun's damaging ultraviolet (UV) radiation. Global ozone levels have dropped across Europe and parts of North America over the last 20 years, and holes in the ozone layer have appeared over both poles. Much of this damage is due to emissions of chlorofluorocarbons (CFCs) and halons, used in car seats, foam cartons, air conditioners, and refrigerants.

The resulting increase in ultraviolet radiation has been linked to the growing incidence of skin cancer. Effects on other species include stresses on marine life and a decline in frog populations. The entire global ecosystem and food chain are affected.

Representatives from 31 nations have agreed to a limit on the production of CFCs. Many U.S. companies originally protested that these chemicals were irreplaceable. But when the government imposed new restrictions, industry rapidly came up with substitutes. In one famous case, they found an alternative that actually saved money—soap and water.

8.3 Global Degradation

Mother Earth is showing signs of stress. Large areas of land have been degraded through overgrazing, deforestation, agricultural mismanagement, and pollution. Some of the results, such as the increased size of desert areas and the loss of rain forest, show up vividly on satellite photographs.

Land degradation is partly the result of human efforts to maximize short-run output with little appreciation of long-run consequences. But it also reflects the desperation of poor people struggling to survive in an increasingly unequal global economy.

In many developing countries, the transition to cash crops and export production has led to increased concentration of land ownership. Rapid population growth has also increased pressures on subsistence farmers.

The earth has only so much "carrying capacity." What we use up, we may never be able to regain.

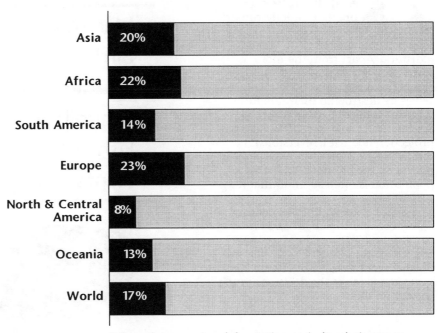

Land degraded* as a percentage of total vegetated land, 1945-91

Region	%
Asia	20%
Africa	22%
South America	14%
Europe	23%
North & Central America	8%
Oceania	13%
World	17%

* through overgrazing, deforestation, agricultural mismanagement, or pollution

8.4 Endangered Species

As we know from dinosaurs, extinction is part of the history of life on earth. But rates of extinction directly caused by human intervention—primarily the destruction of habitat—are alarming. Apart from the moral issues involved, we may be losing species of great potential benefit to ourselves by destroying their habitats.

In this country, the Endangered Species Act provides a safety net of protection against irreversible loss. But by the time an animal or plant is placed on the endangered list, its population is often so small that it cannot be saved.

The Fish and Wildlife Service is currently considering about 3,600 new candidates for the endangered species list. Its resources are quite limited; at its current rate, it would take 50 years just to make the decisions, much less act on them.

Number of endangered species, 1992
(worldwide)

Mammals	307
Birds	226
Reptiles	80
Amphibians	14
Fish	64
Plants	386

8.5 Hazardous Wastes

Many carelessly disposed toxic wastes leak into water supplies underground where they can't be cleaned up. Some are deliberately dumped to avoid the high costs of safe disposal.

Congress created the Superfund in 1980 to solve the problem. But in 1991, the *Washington Post* reported that nearly one-third of the $200 million paid to 45 contractors since 1988 was spent on paperwork and coordination. As of 1991, the Superfund had cleaned up only 63 of the 1,200 sites listed by the Environmental Protection Agency as most threatening.

The biggest hazardous waste problem in the country was created by the government, at the nuclear weapons facility on the Hanford Military Reservation in Washington. There, over 400 billion gallons of radioactive water and liquid wastes were discharged directly into the ground. Experts say it will take at least 30 years and $30 billion to clean it up.

Hazardous waste sites on the National Priority List, 1993

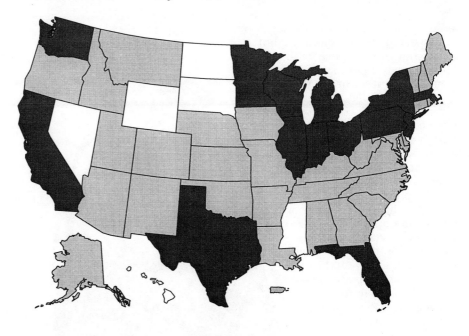

☐ Fewer than 5   ▨ 5-25   ■ More than 25   **Total sites in U.S.: 1,258**

8.6 Mountains of Trash

People generate more garbage than they used to, even though they recycle more. More than 4 pounds per person per day adds up fast, especially in communities that are running out of space for landfills. Containers and packaging alone account for about a third of the volume.

In an effort to reduce trash, many communities now charge by the bag. If disposal gets too expensive, though, some people resort to burning or illegally dumping their trash, which creates a new set of environmental problems. Many communities now require recycling, but there's not always enough industrial demand for recycled materials. Most environmentalists advocate policies that would require producers to use more recycled materials and encourage them to adopt less wasteful packaging.

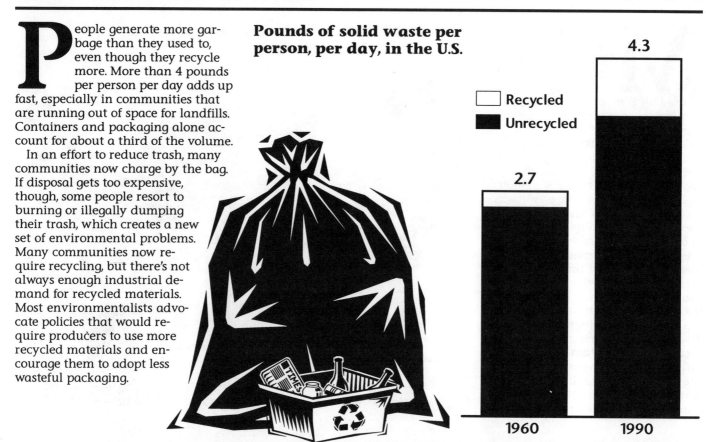

Pounds of solid waste per person, per day, in the U.S.

□ Recycled
■ Unrecycled

4.3

2.7

1960   1990

8.7 Polluted Rivers and Streams

Rivers and streams are cleaner than they used to be. National water quality standards were first established in 1972. Since then, environmental enforcement has paid off. Migratory fish such as shad are beginning to return to previously polluted rivers. Many streams that were once declared off limits are now safe for people to swim in.

But don't jump in just yet. A quarter of the country's rivers and streams remain unsafe. Untreated sewage and industrial effluents used to be the major source of water pollution. But now, the main problem is polluted runoff, particularly from farm chemicals. Since this doesn't come from one specific location, it's harder to pinpoint and regulate.

Between 1988 and 1993, water pollution actually grew worse, partly because the Environmental Protection Agency (EPA) lacked the resources to effectively monitor and enforce the Clean Water Act of 1977.

Percentage of rivers and streams with bacteria counts in violation of EPA standards

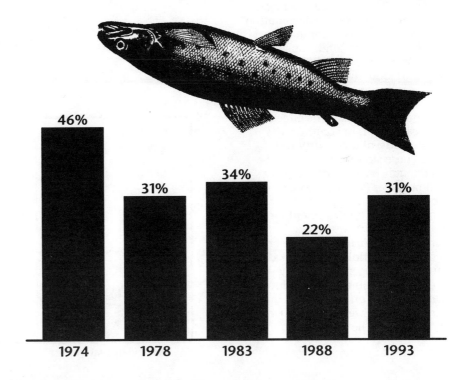

1974	1978	1983	1988	1993
46%	31%	34%	22%	31%

8.8 Bad Stuff in the Air

Warning: Breathing Air May Be Hazardous to Your Health. You don't need a gas mask yet; but in many areas, "air pollution alerts" warn against strenuous exercise when climatic conditions make the air worse than usual.

A recent study of 6 cities shows that air pollution shortens people's lives, making them more prone to lung and heart disease. Its effects were visible even in communities that met federal air pollution standards. These standards may not be high enough, particularly for very small particles (such as those from auto exhaust).

Our country's environmental regulations have successfully reduced the quantity of particulate matter emitted from industrial smokestacks, but sulfur and nitrogen dioxides have increased, contributing to acid rain. Harmful effects on plants and animals have been well documented, particularly in the Northeast.

Air pollutant emissions
(millions of tons)

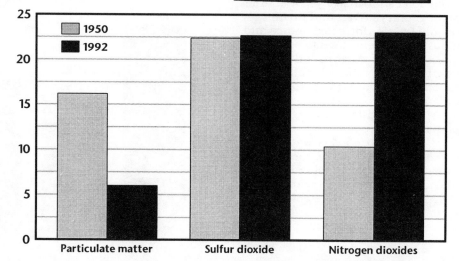

8.9 Energy Hogs

Money buys energy. The richer people are, the more they tend to rely on electricity and gasoline. Citizens of the U.S. consume, on average, an amount of energy equivalent to 22,758 pounds of coal a year, compared with 4,311 for the world as a whole. Most energy comes from limited supplies of fossil fuels, such as oil and coal. But the more significant impact of high energy consumption is environmental: air pollution and hazardous wastes. Fossil fuel combustion also increases emissions of carbon dioxide, which many scientists believe is causing a long-run trend toward global warming. Continued heavy energy consumption in industrialized countries could bring about climatic changes particularly threatening to farmers in developing countries, whose lives depend on patterns of temperature and rain.

A treaty signed in Rio de Janeiro in 1992 calls for countries to develop "climate plans" and reduce energy use. Whether they will effectively do so or not remains to be seen.

Energy consumption in the U.S., 1991
(in pounds of coal equivalent per capita)

World 4,467

U.S. 23,810

THE U.S., WITH 5% OF THE WORLD'S *POPULATION*, USES 25% OF THE WORLD'S *ENERGY* AND EMITS 22% OF *ALL CO₂ PRODUCED*...

WELL--WE'RE *AMERICANS*! PROFLIGATE CONSUMPTION OF THE PLANET'S NATURAL RESOURCES IS OUR *BIRTHRIGHT*!

SUPPORT THE TROOPS

Tom Tomorrow

8.10 The Price Is Wrong

Energy is not cheap. It only seems that way. Right now, the oil-exporting countries are in a weak position, which helps keep oil import prices down. More important, the price of fossil fuels doesn't reflect the hidden costs that their use inflicts on the environment. You may pay only $1.20 a gallon for gasoline, or 10 cents a kilowatt-hour for electricity; but sooner or later, you or your children will suffer the ill effects of the air pollution, radioactive wastes, and other "externalities" created.

What would happen to prices of fossil fuels if estimates of these environmental costs were added in? Gasoline would cost 40% more. Electricity from existing coal-fired plants (the source of acid rain problems) would cost 100% more.

Higher prices, of course, would encourage people to economize, but industry opposition to such increases is intense. And many consumers would rather save money today than worry about environmental costs down the road. In response to this problem, Congress passed the National Energy Policy Act (NEPA) in 1992. It encourages some forms of conservation but ignores gasoline consumption and reduces public participation in the licensing of nuclear power plants. In other words, NEPA does little to compensate for the misleading impact of cheap energy prices.

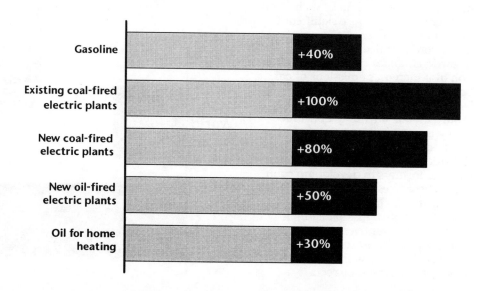

Energy price increases when environmental costs are added

- Gasoline: +40%
- Existing coal-fired electric plants: +100%
- New coal-fired electric plants: +80%
- New oil-fired electric plants: +50%
- Oil for home heating: +30%

8.11 Free Market Environmentalism

Many environmentalists argue that the key to good policy is setting prices that reflect the true costs imposed on society as a whole. Sometimes the market does a better job at this than public policy. For instance:

> **By subsidizing radioactive waste disposal** and limiting private liability in the event of an accident, the federal government artificially lowers the cost of nuclear power.

> **Federal subsidies** to ranching and timber interests encourage overuse. Many ranchers in the West pay $1.86 a month to graze a cow and calf on federal land, while grazing rights on private land adjacent to federal tracts cost $9.

Some environmentalists advocate letting companies buy and sell pollution "permits," rather than setting uniform regulations.

> **If such permits are carefully designed** and sufficiently expensive, they may give firms a strong incentive to reduce pollution in an economically efficient way.

> **Tradable pollution permits** are now being allocated to electric utilities. The effects remain to be seen.

8.12 Man-made Disasters

1990, Persian Gulf:.

More than 80 Kuwaiti oil wells, sabotaged by retreating Iraqi troops, created the largest oil spill in history. Resulting fires produced roughly 10 times as much air pollution as that generated by all U.S. industrial and power-generating plants in a year.

1989, Prince William Sound, Alaska:

When the oil tanker *Exxon Valdez* ran aground, it leaked about 250,000 barrels of crude oil into the sea. The cleanup, which was only partially successful, cost about $2.5 billion. Exxon paid $1 billion in civil and criminal penalties but faces a possible $15 billion in punitive damages.

1986, Chernobyl, Ukraine:

A core meltdown at a large nuclear reactor allowed radiation to escape. Almost 50,000 people were evacuated. By official count, 31 people died; some claim that mortality was actually in the thousands. The total cost is unknown.

1984, Bhopal, India:

When a Union Carbide plant released 42 tons of poisonous gas into the atmosphere, 2,500 people died in the first week and another 500,000 were injured. In 1989, the Indian government negotiated a legal settlement of $470 million; but as of August 1993, only $3.1 million had been paid by Union Carbide.

8.13 The EPA Is Weak

The Environmental Protection Agency (EPA) needs protection itself. Underfinancing and understaffing make it difficult to enforce the nation's environmental laws, much less develop new ones. In 1980, the EPA's total expenditures amounted to a mere 0.9% of the federal budget. Since then, they have declined to about 0.4%. Over the same time period, real spending fell from $9.5 billion to $6.3 billion. President Clinton's 1994 budget imposed further cuts, though it increased outlays for the National Aeronautics and Space Administration (NASA), an agency about the same size as the EPA.

The country's environmental legislation is a complicated patchwork, and many critics argue that the EPA is too vulnerable to political mood swings. Congress occasionally uses it as a pork barrel, supporting specific projects to please constituents. The EPA could function better if comprehensive legislation allowed it to set priorities for dealing with the most serious problems first.

Environmental Protection Agency budget as percentage of total federal budget

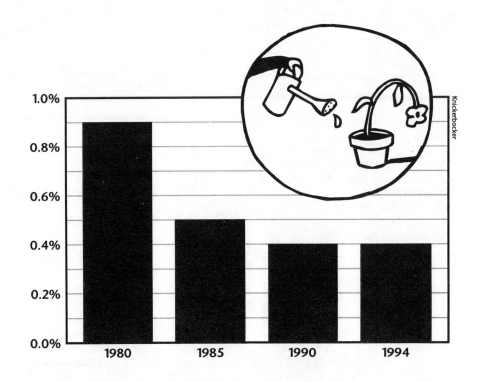

Knickerbocker

8.14 The Antipollution Industry

Knickerbocker

Spending on pollution control is an investment in the future of the environment. Strict regulations and stiff fines can make such investments profitable: Business expenditures are much greater than those made by the government or consumers. After a small dip in the early 1980s, when enforcement was lax, businesses began to spend more and more on pollution control.

Environmental regulations do not necessarily slow growth or lower employment. The antipollution industry, which includes the manufacture of scrubbers for industrial smokestacks and catalytic converters for automobiles, is generating both jobs and profits.

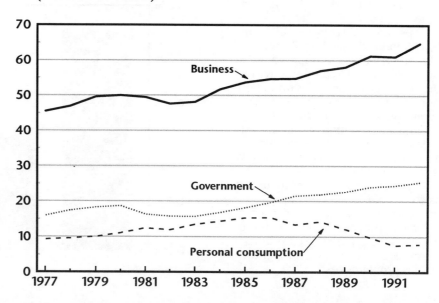

Total expenditures on pollution abatement
(billions of $1992)

Business

Government

Personal consumption

Knickerbocker

8.15 Environmental Racism

People of color are more likely than whites to live in communities with air pollution, toxic waste, and other environmental hazards.

 In 1990, 437 cities and counties failed to meet at least one of the Environmental Protection Agency's ambient air quality standards; 57% of whites, 65% of African-Americans, and 80% of Latinos lived in these areas.

 Although class plays an important role in the location of commercial hazardous waste sites, race is even more significant. In the late 1980s, 3 out of every 5 African-Americans and Latinos lived in communities with uncontrolled toxic waste sites.

 All nuclear bomb test sites on the U.S. mainland are on Native American land. More than 3 dozen reservations have been targeted for landfills and incinerators.

8.16 Exporting Hazards

"I think the economic logic behind dumping a load of toxic waste in the lowest-wage country is impeccable, and we should face up to it."

Laurence Summers, Chief Economist, World Bank, 1991

Exporting Waste

In the 1980s, both the U.S. and the European Economic Community tightened regulations on the disposal of hazardous waste. As a result, many companies tried to sneak their wastes into poor countries where they could be secretly disposed of. Every industrialized country except the U.S. now favors an outright ban on hazardous waste exports.

Recycled Hazards

Also worrisome are routine shipments of recyclable but dangerous leftovers such as lead batteries, oil contaminated with polychlorinated biphenyls (PCBs), and old equipment containing asbestos. These are routinely sold to companies in countries that lack environmental or worker protection laws and can therefore process such items cheaply.

Border Export Zones

Booming areas along the Mexican border tend to ignore environmental regulations as long as jobs are being created. The New River, which flows from Mexico into California's Imperial Valley, is one of the most polluted rivers in the world.

Chapter 9 **Macroeconomics**

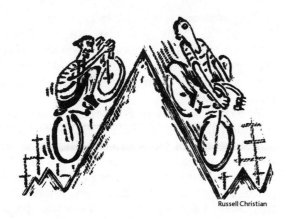

Russell Christian

Macroeconomics, or "macro" for short, looks at the economy as a whole. Its main focus is economic growth: increase in the Gross Domestic Product, or the total value of the goods and services produced in the country. Over the last 20 years, economic growth in the U.S. has slowed. This chapter looks at some of the reasons why.

It is important to distinguish long-run trends from the ups and downs of the business cycle. *Chart 9.1* demonstrates the cyclical nature of economic growth. During a recession, the value of output declines; during a recovery, it increases. *Chart 9.2* illustrates some of the forces behind these ups and downs.

Chart 9.3 documents the decline in growth rates since the 1960s. One big problem is slow productivity growth, pictured in *Chart 9.4*. Despite generous tax breaks and low wage costs, U.S. firms did not invest much in the late 1980s and early 1990s (*Chart 9.5*).

Sometimes low investment is blamed on low savings. But business savings seem more than adequate, even though personal savings have declined (see *Chart 9.6*). The real culprit may be the high interest rates pictured in *Chart 9.7*, which deter investment. What determines interest rates? The most important influence is Federal Reserve Board policy. *Chart 9.8* explains some of the factors that enter into the Fed's decisions.

The 1980s witnessed an unprecedented wave of corporate takeovers. As international competition intensified, many U.S. corporations chose to buy new companies instead of improving their own productive capacity (*Chart 9.9*). This restructuring helped their own balance sheets more than the economy as a whole. It also increased corporate indebtedness. Interest payments began to consume a higher percentage of profits (*Chart 9.10*). Not surprisingly, many firms were unable to stay afloat. As *Chart 9.11* demonstrates, the business failure rate soared. Small businesses were particularly vulnerable.

Financial pressures, combined with deregulation, battered the banking sector of the economy. *Chart 9.12* summarizes the cost of bailing out failed savings and loan associations. Commercial banks have also gone through precarious periods (*Chart 9.13*). They can afford to take financial risks because many of their deposits are insured by the federal government.

The burden of debt is a drag on many American households. In 1992, they owed, on average, almost a whole year's income (see *Chart 9.14*). But people can't live off plastic forever. Those who are financially overextended tend to be cautious consumers, even when an economic recovery gets under way.

Corporations have also been running into trouble. Perhaps the single most important indicator of success in a capitalist economy is the rate of return on corporate investments. As *Chart 9.15* shows, the after-tax profit rate has declined in spite of cuts in corporate taxes.

Are these trends worth worrying about? You wouldn't think so if you merely looked at the Dow Jones average of stock prices, which has soared in recent years (see *Chart 9.16*). But the relationship between the economy's actual performance and the prices of corporate stocks is tenuous. In early 1994, the news of economic recovery actually spooked the stock market, leaving some economists to wonder whether what's good for the Dow Jones is good for the U.S. as a whole.

9.1 The Ups and Downs of GDP

We produce a lot of stuff in this country, about six trillion dollars worth. The value of all goods and services bought and sold, or gross domestic product (GDP), is not a very good measure of standards of living, but it does provide an indicator of overall growth that is important for understanding the dynamics of unemployment and inflation.

The ups and downs of GDP reflect the business cycle. Years of rapid expansion are followed by periods of recession (negative economic growth), followed in turn by economic recovery. When businesses have a hard time selling their products, they hire fewer workers and often lay off some, increasing unemployment. Periods of rapid recovery, on the other hand, can lead to inflation.

Policy makers try to influence the business cycle by changing interest rates and the level of government spending. But they can seldom predict what the exact consequences of their actions will be.

Russell Christian

Growth and growth rate of GDP, 1950-94
(gray bars indicate recession periods)

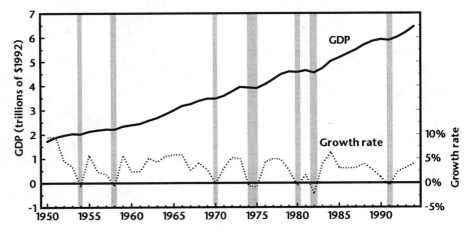

9.2 The Business Cycle

An increase in real wages almost always threatens profits, and the relationship between wages, profits, and unemployment helps explain the business cycle. When profits are high, firms have an incentive to expand and hire more workers. But lower unemployment can eventually lead to higher wages and lower profits.

When profits fall, firms tend to lay off workers or to relocate to areas with lower wages. The resulting unemployment may then lower wages and restore profitability and economic growth. But if wages get too low, workers can't afford to buy what is produced. Unless demand is increased some other way, a recession can develop. Increased profits don't necessarily lead to increased economic growth within the U.S. because they may be invested overseas.

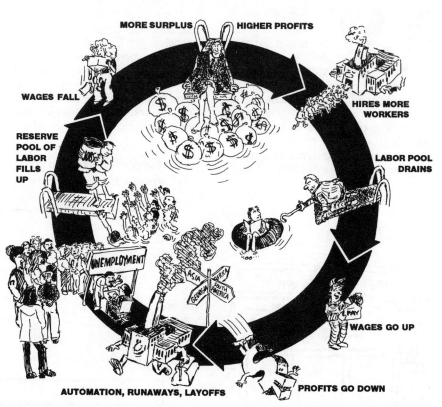

MORE SURPLUS   HIGHER PROFITS

WAGES FALL

HIRES MORE WORKERS

RESERVE POOL OF LABOR FILLS UP

LABOR POOL DRAINS

UNEMPLOYMENT

WAGES GO UP

AUTOMATION, RUNAWAYS, LAYOFFS

PROFITS GO DOWN

Howard Saunders

9.3 Declining Growth Rates

L ooking back, the 1950s and 1960s seem like wonder years. The average annual rate of growth in GDP was over 3½%. People had a sense that their hard work was paying off and their lives were getting better.

In the 1970s, things began to seem more difficult. Prices went up fast, but unemployment also surged. Slower growth meant that there was less to go around. After deep recessions in the early 1980s, growth seemed to be picking up, but the overall average for the decade was pretty low. And because income inequality intensified, the benefits from growth were unevenly distributed.

The recession of 1990 got this decade off to a slow start. In 1993 and 1994, the economy began to improve. But the recovery has a long way to go before ordinary people will feel it.

Knickerbocker

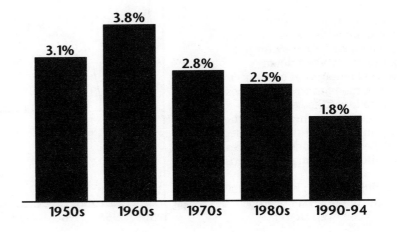

Average annual growth rate of real GDP, by decade

1950s	1960s	1970s	1980s	1990-94
3.1%	3.8%	2.8%	2.5%	1.8%

9.4 Productivity Slowdown

The driving force of economic growth is higher productivity, or output per labor hour. New technology, better equipment, greater skills, and improved methods of organization can make it possible to produce more with less. But new technology alone doesn't seem to do the trick.

Although more computers and electronic gadgets are available to consumers, the rate of productivity growth among workers has declined. In some years, such as 1989, output per hour actually went down.

Increased competition and uncertainty have made many companies reluctant to invest heavily in new equipment. On the other hand, productivity improvements in some sectors of the economy, such as services, may not show up in aggregate statistics.

Productivity growth has been slow. But the rate of growth of average wages has been even slower.

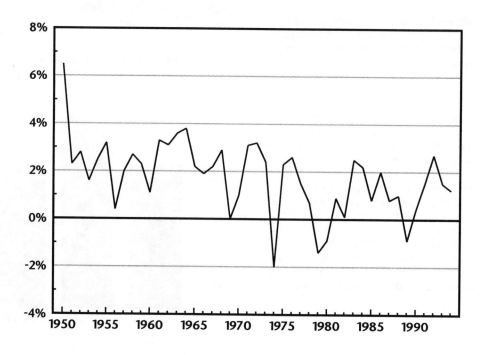

Percentage change in output per hour, 1950-94
(nonfarm business sector)

9.5 Less Investment

If you want higher productivity, you generally have to pay for it. Nonresidential investment provides a good indicator of efforts to increase future output. Measured as a percentage of net domestic product, it reflects the ups and downs of the business cycle but shows a recent downward trend.

The tax cuts implemented by the Reagan administration in 1981 were meant to encourage investment. But as the saying goes, "You can lead a horse to water, but you can't make him drink." High interest rates, among other factors, had a deterrent effect. Many corporations chose either to invest overseas or to spend money buying out other firms, rather than actually increase productive capacity.

In the early 1990s, expenditures on producers' durable equipment, the most important subcategory of nonresidential investment, were less than 2% of output.

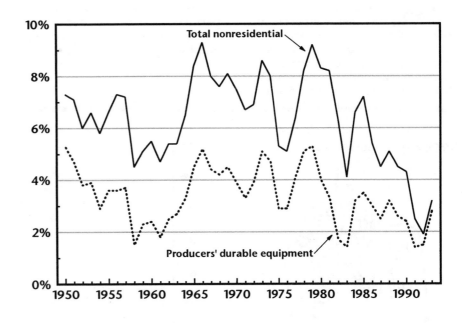

Investment as a percentage of output*

* net fixed investment of nonfinancial corporations relative to their net domestic product

9.6 Too Little Savings?

Russell Christian

Are Americans just careless spendthrifts who deserve the blame for all their own economic woes? Conservative pundits often suggest as much. By their account, if people would just save more money, interest rates would go down and investment would go up.

But that view is far too simple. It is true that personal savings in the U.S. are low as a percentage of GDP. But the bulk of all savings (about 70%) comes from businesses, which have maintained a relatively high rate.

Personal savings have declined partly because wages have declined and people are struggling to maintain their former standard of living.

Russell Christian

Savings as a percentage of GDP, 1950-94

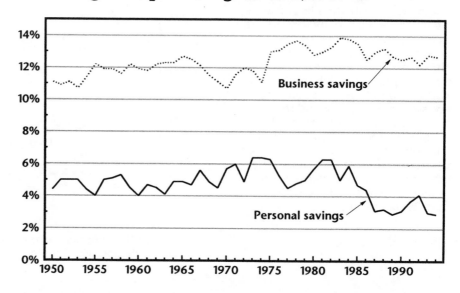

9.7 The Cost of Borrowing

Corporations usually borrow money to invest, so they pay close attention to something called the "real interest rate." They take the nominal rate of interest quoted by banks and subtract the expected inflation rate because inflation allows borrowers to repay loans with dollars that have lost some of their value.

In the mid-1970s, inflation was so high that the real interest rate was actually negative. When inflation declined in the early 1980s, the nominal interest rate didn't decline nearly as fast. As a result, the real interest rate reached unprecedented levels. This made some people (those with a lot of money in the bank) quite happy, but it deterred investment.

By the 1990s, real interest rates had fallen, encouraging investment and economic recovery. But in 1994, the Federal Reserve Board, more fearful of inflation than of unemployment, decided they should be increased again.

Nominal and real interest rates
(corporate bonds rated Aaa)

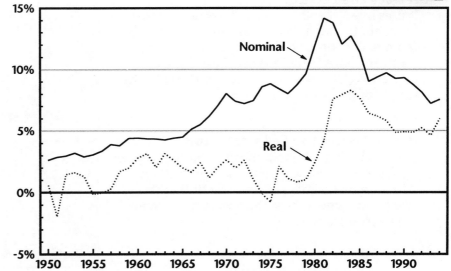

9.8 The Story Behind Interest Rates

Who determines them?

The Fed, a.k.a. the Board of Governors of the Federal Reserve System, a group of bankers appointed by the president for 14-year terms, makes decisions that influence interest rates. Alan Greenspan has been the head of the Fed since 1987.

What does the Fed do?

It uses interest rates to steer the economy, raising them to induce recessions and lowering them to encourage economic growth. As the "bankers' bank," the Fed can change the rate of interest it charges its members and modify the supply of money in various ways.

What determines the Fed's decisions?

The Fed is supposed to buffer the business cycle and help the economy as a whole. But many critics argue that its policies benefit bankers and bond owners more than workers by keeping interest rates too high.

Does the deficit raise interest rates?

A big government deficit may encourage the Fed to increase rates, but there is no necessary connection between the two. In 1994, the Fed raised interest rates sharply despite a falling deficit.

9.9 More Mergers

The 1980s saw a huge increase in merger and buyout activity. Rather than investing in new plants and equipment, many corporations began to buy out their competition. When the Reagan administration relaxed the standards of antitrust law and cut tax rates, many corporations decided they could make more money by diversifying than by expanding their own productive capacity.

In theory, takeover threats are supposed to increase the efficiency of corporations by putting more pressure on management to perform (or lose their jobs). But most mergers have increased corporate debt without showing much productivity gain. Even companies that avoided takeovers were affected; some took "poison pills," a cute name for loads of debt designed to make them seem less attractive to potential suitors.

OUR LATEST BUYOUT AIDS THE EFFICIENCY OF THE MARKET

IT EXPRESSES THE TRUE GENIUS OF CAPITALIST ENTERPRISE

BUT HOW CAN WE HANDLE ALL THE DEBT WE TOOK ON?

FIRE THE EMPLOYEES AND SELL OFF THE PLANTS!

WASSERMAN © '90 BOSTON GLOBE DIST. BY L.A. TIMES SYND.

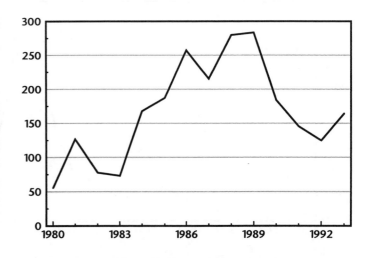

Value of mergers and buyouts
(billions of $1992)

9.10 More Debt, More Interest

U.S. corporations struggled under a growing burden of debt in the 1980s, when interest payments averaged about 83% of profits, compared with only about 9% in the 1950s. If borrowed money is spent wisely, interest payments are just a cost of doing business. But when companies incur debt that doesn't enable them to increase their profits, they run into trouble.

The increased financial pressures of the 1980s led many corporations to postpone investments, cut into "expendables" such as research and development, sell off profitable assets, and/or lay off large numbers of workers. Some companies just went belly up.

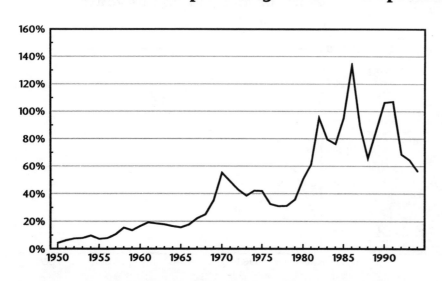

Net interest as a percentage of after-tax profits

Russel Christian

9.11 Business Failures

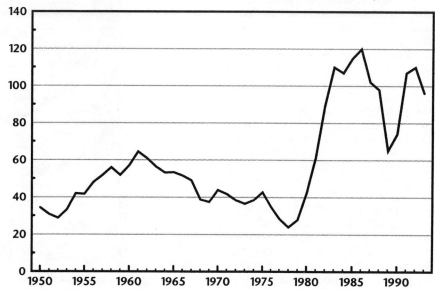

The probusiness decade didn't quite deliver what it promised. The business failure rate increased sharply in the 1980s, reaching a post-Depression high of 120 per 10,000 firms in 1986.

High interest rates were the major source of stress. The Federal Reserve Board, preoccupied with fighting inflation, kept interest rates high, leaving small businesses, in particular, to fend for themselves. But even big businesses ran into trouble. Many who borrowed heavily for mergers and acquisitions found it difficult to sustain their cash flow.

Failure rate per 10,000 businesses

Knickerbocker

9.12 The Savings and Loan Bailout

In the early 1980s, when interest rates skyrocketed as a result of inflation and restrictive monetary policy, many savings and loan associations (S&Ls), stuck with large amounts of low-interest home mortgages, ran into trouble. Instead of moving in to close the troubled institutions, policymakers chose to deregulate and increase federal deposit insurance from $30,000 to $100,000 per account.

With weak supervision and deposits insured by taxpayers, most S&L's engaged in an unprecedented wave of speculation in an attempt to make up for past losses. More than 1,500 thrift institutions failed. The belated bailout will cost in excess of $200 billion: more than the federal government spent on both the AFDC and the Food Stamps programs in the 1980's, 3 times as much as all government support to health research during the Reagan and Bush administrations, and 5 times the cost of repairing the nation's 240,000 deficient bridges.

Adding insult to injury, the Resolution Trust Corporation (RTC), set up to liquidate failed institutions' assets, sold them at bargain-basement prices to big players at the expense of small local lending institutions. Ten banks bought over half of the deposits from failed S&L's.

9.13 Problem Banks

I s another expensive public bailout on the way? Like savings and loan associations, commercial banks have been facing increased competition from other financial institutions. In the 1980s, most tried to compensate for declining profit margins by taking greater risks, lending to takeover artists, property developers, and foreign governments. When many of these loans failed, hundreds of banks were left in a precarious position.

As of 1991, nearly 1,500 banks with assets of more than $1 trillion were, for all practical purposes, insolvent. Banks are required to hold capital as a buffer against loan losses; those with low ratios are more vulnerable to defaults on loans. Some of the country's largest banks reported capital/assets ratios well below the 5.5% required by federal regulation.

Falling interest rates helped banks improve their profit margins and stock prices. But their periodic vulnerability raises questions about the stability of the banking system.

Assets and capital asset ratios of top 10 problem banks, 1991 (billions of $1991)

Bank	Assets	Ratio*
Citicorp	$216,922	-0.5%
Chase Manhattan	$98,197	1.2%
Wells Fargo & Co.	$53,547	2.2%
C&S/Sovran Corp.	$47,968	2.2%
Bank of Boston Corp.	$32,700	2.3%
Shawmut Nat. Corp.	$22,832	1.4%
Midlantic Corp.	$18,170	-3.6%
MNC Financial Inc.	$17,461	-2.0%
Marine Midland	$16,947	0.9%
UJB Financial Corp.	$13,384	2.8%

*average of estimates

9.14 Deeper in Debt

The average American household now owes just about as much money as it earns in a year. As a result, when someone loses a job, they also risk losing their car or their home.

Household debt increased considerably as a percentage of after-tax income in the 1980s. Affluent families borrowed in order to speculate in real estate and financial markets, but many low- and middle-income families resorted to more debt to compensate for declining wages.

When interest rates went up, many families couldn't make their payments. The rate of delinquency on mortgage loans doubled in the 1980s, as did the rate of personal bankruptcies.

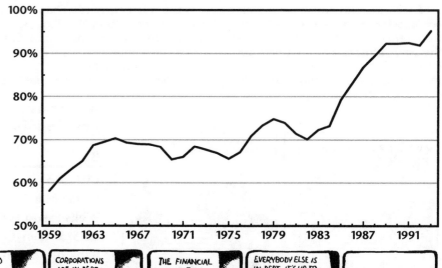

Household debt as a percentage of after-tax income, 1959-92

9.15 Sagging Corporate Profit Rates

Has the golden age of U.S. capitalism come to an end? The profit rate has always had its ups and downs. But since the high-flying 1960s, it has been mostly on the downside.

The before-tax profit rate slid steadily downward in the 1970s. The after-tax profit rate didn't fall as much because of cuts in corporate income taxes. The difference between the two rates was far smaller in 1992 than in 1965.

In the 1980s, oil prices stabilized, inflation subsided, real wages stagnated, and the federal government loosened regulations. But interest rates remained high, and international competition intensified, keeping profit margins low. The economic recovery of 1993-94 perked profits up a bit. Where they will go from here, nobody knows.

Nicole Hollander

Profits of nonfinancial corporations as a percentage of capital stock, 1950-93

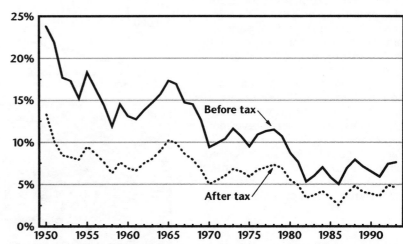

9.16 Keeping Up with the Dow Jones

A lot of people made a lot of money in the stock market in the 1980s and early 1990s. The Dow Jones, a common index of industrial stock prices, kept going up and up. A wave of hostile takeovers and insider trading kept Wall Street unusually busy. It also made some people unusually rich.

Increases in stock prices reflect optimism about the future and sometimes serve as a "leading indicator" of economic trends. But stock prices say little about the actual performance of the economy or its ability to deliver improvements in standards of living.

In 1994, good news about faster growth, higher profits, and more jobs actually slowed the growth of the Dow Jones because some investors began worrying about inflation. People who speculate in stocks and bonds generally pay more attention to financial indicators than to the underlying health of the economy.

Dow Jones industrial average, 1950-94

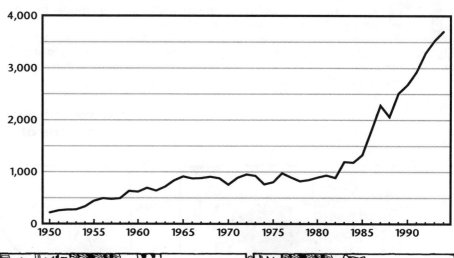

Experts BLAMe yesterday's drop in the Dow on poor Corporate earnings...

AND Jupiter in Retrograde.

Chapter 10 **The Global Economy**

Once upon a time, in the aftermath of World War II, the U.S. economy enjoyed unquestioned dominance; U.S. firms faced little competition from overseas. This is no longer the case. Increased world trade, lower tariff barriers, and greater capital mobility have taught U.S. firms some humility. They have also weakened the influence of the nation-state. Just because a corporation is based in the U.S. doesn't mean that most of its stockholders, or even most of its workers, live here.

A genuine appreciation of "globalization" is key to understanding current economic trends. This chapter focuses on three issues: the U.S. compared with its chief competitors, new patterns of trade, and continuing problems of underdevelopment.

The U.S. no longer has the highest GDP per capita in the world, as Chart 10.1 indicates. The reason is fairly obvious—Japanese firms, in particular, are now more productive than U.S. firms in a variety of industries (see *Chart 10.2*).

In the long run, the country that invests the most grows the fastest. Japan is out in front of the pack, with higher rates of investment relative to GDP than either the U.S. or Germany (see *Chart 10.3*). Of course, quality matters as much as, if not more than, quantity. Civilian research and development is a priority because it can generate technological breakthroughs. U.S. firms look rather complacent on this score relative to their counterparts in Germany and Japan (see *Chart 10.4*).

For the last 30 years, the U.S. has imported more than it has exported. The U.S. still exports more services than it imports. But for the first time since 1914, U.S. citizens receive less income from their investments overseas than foreigners send home from their investments in this country (see *Chart 10.5*).

Even sectors in which U.S. corporations still have the edge are running into problems. This country is still the center of the world computer industry. But many firms engage in "outsourcing," commissioning the production of labor-intensive components overseas. As a result, we have recently become net importers of computers and related equipment (see *Chart 10.6*).

What are the factors that motivate firms to relocate overseas? Cheap wages are important, but they don't tell the whole story. As *Chart 10.7* emphasizes, the countries from which we currently import the most actually have higher wages than we do. Productivity matters. So does proximity to markets. So far, most U.S. foreign investment goes to Europe and Canada, where consumers have a lot of money to spend (see *Chart 10.8*).

While the relative position of the U.S. seems to be declining, most U.S. corporations are getting a larger share of their profits from overseas, between 15% and 20% in the early 1990s (see *Chart 10.9*). Meanwhile, what's happening to the recipients of U.S. foreign investment? Historically, countries have lost more than they have gained: Profit outflow has exceeded investment inflow. *Chart 10.10* shows that situation has changed because so much money is now being invested overseas.

What has been the impact of increased trade and foreign investment on the world's poorest people? As *Chart 10.11* illustrates, global inequalities are extreme. And while some regions of the developing world, notably China and East Asia, now enjoy higher per capita income than they did in 1980, others are worse off. Sub-Saharan Africa, in particular, is suffering (see *Chart 10.12*).

A focus on conventional measures of growth can be quite misleading. Much depends on how goods and services are distributed. *Chart 10.13* points out that some relatively rich countries such as Saudi Arabia actually have higher infant mortality levels than relatively poor but egalitarian regimes such as Sri Lanka and Costa Rica. *Chart 10.14* documents the continuing extent of world hunger, manifested in the percentage of children who are underweight.

Developing countries cannot simply assume that world trade will carry them to prosperity. Countries that depend on exports of a single raw material (often an economic legacy of the colonial era) have been and remain in a vulnerable position (see *Chart 10.15*). And all nations need to be aware of the potential burden of debt. *Chart 10.16* shows that over the past decade, developing nations collectively spent more on paying back old loans than they got in new ones.

10.1 No Longer Number One

The U.S. is losing ground. Boosted by greater rates of productivity increase, Japan and Germany have gradually increased their gross domestic product per capita relative to ours. After 1985, Japan surpassed Germany, becoming our most important competitor.

The U.S. has much to gain from economic growth in other countries. But their superior performance raises questions about our own relatively slow rate of growth. America's heyday lasted from the end of the Second World War to 1973, when GDP per capita doubled over the span of 25 years. No wonder, since high rates of investment increased output per worker at a healthy rate of 2.8% per year. Since 1973, productivity growth has slowed to about 1% a year.

Other countries, such as Japan, have increased productivity faster. The U.S. should try to learn from their example.

Gross domestic product per capita, relative to the U.S.

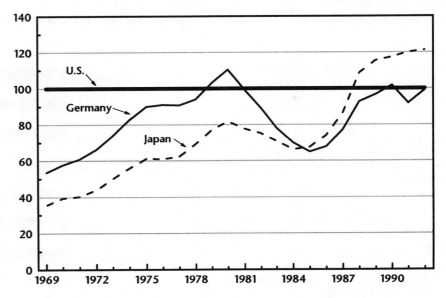

10.2 Who's Best at What?

Labor productivity offers a yardstick for international competitiveness in individual industries. The country that uses labor most efficiently in producing a particular good can usually produce that good at the lowest price and therefore sell more of it than other countries.

The U.S. once set the standard for key manufacturing sectors, but no longer. Japan has a 15% to 45% productivity advantage over both Germany and the U.S. in automobiles, metalworking, consumer electronics, and steel. Germany matches U.S. productivity in steel and metalworking and surpasses Japan in food. The United States still has the highest overall average, partly because of its comparative advantage in food production.

These differences in labor productivity partly reflect levels of investment in new technology. But they are also related to product design and workplace organization. Japanese firms encourage cooperation and pay top managers far less relative to workers than U.S. firms.

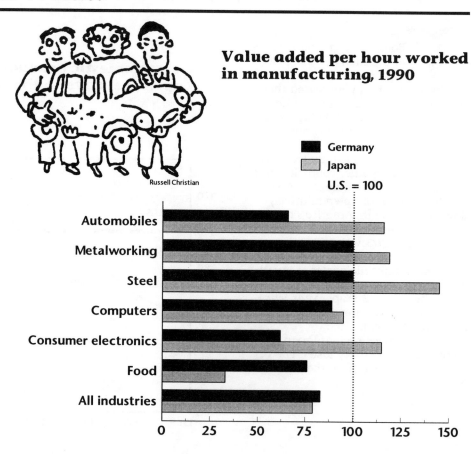

Russell Christian

Value added per hour worked in manufacturing, 1990

Germany
Japan

U.S. = 100

Automobiles
Metalworking
Steel
Computers
Consumer electronics
Food
All industries

0 25 50 75 100 125 150

10.3 Who Invests the Most?

Small wonder that Japanese products now set the standard for quality in many industries. U.S. corporations grew complacent in the 1950s, while Japanese corporations invested quite aggressively. Since 1962, Japan has spent about twice as large a share of its GDP on investment as the U.S. Most Japanese workers now combine their energies with more and better tools than their American counterparts.

Since the early 1980s, the investment share of U.S. output has actually declined. Some economists argue that the structure of our capital markets encourages investors to seek short-term "paper gains" rather than long-run improvements in efficiency. While 70% of Japanese stock is held by permanent owners for the long term, 60% of U.S. stock is owned by investors who buy and sell quite frequently.

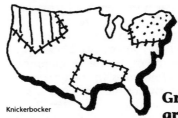

Knickerbocker

Gross investment as a percentage of gross domestic product, 1962-92

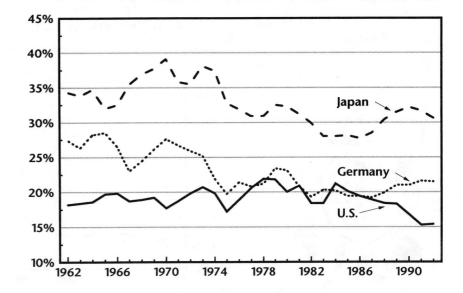

10.4 Losing the High-Tech Race

Where do new productive technologies come from? Sometimes they are discovered by accident, but usually they are the result of a sustained commitment to research and development (R&D). Partly because of its preoccupation with military research, the U.S. has long lagged behind Japan and Germany in the share of GDP it devotes to nonmilitary R&D. In recent years, however, the gap has substantially increased.

The wave of mergers and "restructuring" of the 1980s increased the burden of debt on many corporations and may have discouraged private investments in the development of new technologies. In the words of a representative of the National Association of Manufacturers, "R&D has higher risks and longer-term payoffs than most expenditures; it's a highly postponable item—a handy target for cost-cutters."

Foreign corporations are winning an increasing proportion of U.S. patents. In 1992, three Japanese corporations topped the list: Canon, Hitachi, and Toshiba.

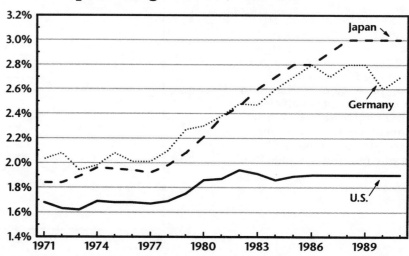

Civilian research and development as a percentage of GNP, 1971-91

10.5 Imbalance of Trade

To paraphrase a toy maker, Imports "R" Us. The U.S. buys a lot more merchandise from other countries than they buy from us. Even though we enjoy a positive balance of trade in services and investment income, these are not enough to compensate for the excess of imports over exports.

This merchandise deficit doesn't matter much as long as people overseas don't mind holding the dollars we pay them for imports (even though there's little they want to buy with them). But the imbalance of trade contributes to instability in the value of the dollar, which makes it hard to predict how much imports will cost in the future.

According to traditional economic theory, a decrease in the value of the dollar should automatically lower the trade deficit by making imports more expensive and lowering the price of U.S. exports. But almost half of U.S. imports come from foreign affiliates of U.S. firms and are therefore not very sensitive to currency fluctuations.

Outflows minus inflows of foreign trade
(billions of $1992)

Russell Christian

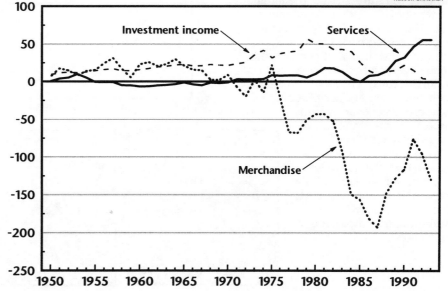

10.6 Made in America?

As *Fortune* put it in 1994, "The U.S. is winning, but it's a hollow victory." The appearance of competitive success masks an underlying weakness.

U.S. firms saw their share of the global market for personal computers rise from 59% in 1985 to 70% in 1992. But over the same period, the foreign content of U.S.-made computers rose from 10% to 30%. Most systems include imported peripherals (such as printers) and imported components (such as monitors, disk drives, and flat panel displays). The result: Net exports of computers, peripherals, and components (exports minus imports) have declined considerably since 1980.

Computers are more of a growth industry for investors than for workers: While the total value of shipments rose 12% from 1987 to 1993, total industry employment fell by 30%.

Net exports of computers, peripherals, and components (billions of $1992)

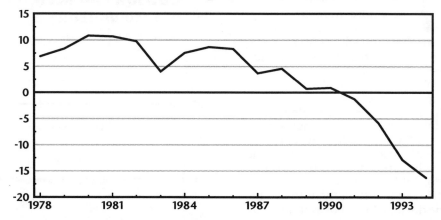

10.7 Trade Without Borders

Two major agreements designed to lower barriers to trade and international investment were recently approved by the U.S. government. Both promise to promote growth and efficiency but threaten loss of national control over social, economic, and environmental policy.

NAFTA, the North American Free Trade Agreement, approved in 1993, created a "free trade area" that now includes the U.S., Canada, and Mexico and may be extended to other Latin American countries. Tariffs and restrictions on international investment have been lowered within the region. Critics point out that the agreement lacks the social protections that similar trading blocs, such as the European Economic Community (EEC), have put in place.

GATT, the General Agreement on Tariffs and Trade, approved in 1994, now governs about 90% of world trade. Its rules require consistent policies toward all signatory countries (except free trade areas) and elimination of nontariff barriers, such as restrictions on imports whose production violates fair labor and environmental standards. The agreement also establishes a World Trade Organization (WTO) to resolve trade disputes.

10.8 Cheap Labor and Trade

"A giant sucking sound," Ross Perot predicted, would be heard when passage of the North American Free Trade Agreement (NAFTA) sent manufacturing jobs down the drain. Is anybody listening? NAFTA made it easier for U.S. firms to move to Mexico in search of cheap labor, but its actual effects may not be felt for years.

Many factors other than cheap labor influence international flows of capital and trade. Currently, the U.S. imports more from high-wage countries such as Japan, Canada, and Germany than from low-wage countries like Mexico and Korea. On average, workers from "competing" nations were paid only slightly less than U.S. workers in 1992: $15.46 per hour compared with $16.17.

Political stability and public infrastructure, as well as a high level of education, often compensate for high wage costs. If low-wage countries begin to provide these amenities, they will make greater inroads.

Hourly labor costs in U.S. and major trading partners, 1992 (in $US)

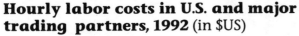

Mexico	$2.35
Korea	$4.93
Taiwan	$5.19
Japan	$16.16
U.S.	$16.17
Canada	$17.02
Germany	$25.94

10.9 Where Do U.S. Corporations Invest?

U.S. corporations roam the globe in search of opportunities to maximize profits. While cheap labor is always a factor, access to the markets (and the pocketbooks) of affluent countries has historically been more important. In 1992, Europe and Canada received 63% of all U.S. investment abroad, compared with only 26% for all developing nations combined.

Corporations based in other countries find the U.S. attractive for similar reasons. They now invest almost as much here as U.S. corporations invest abroad.

But the pattern of international direct investment may be changing. Since 1980, the five fastest-growing recipients of U.S. direct investment (apart from Japan) have been the low-wage Asian economies of Taiwan, China, Thailand, South Korea, and Singapore.

Location of U.S. foreign investment, 1992

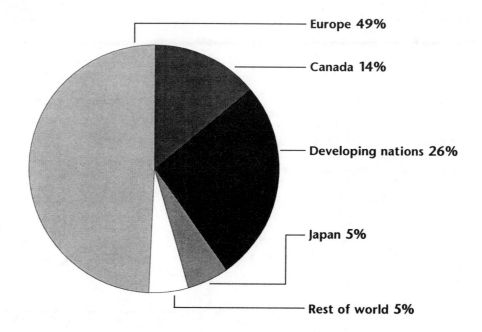

Europe 49%

Canada 14%

Developing nations 26%

Japan 5%

Rest of world 5%

10.10 More Profits from Overseas

Knickerbocker

The more profits U.S. corporations earn in other countries, the less they need to worry about infrastructure and education in this country. Small wonder, then, that they seem to be worrying less and less. In 1993, $63 billion (or 16% of all before-tax corporate profits) came from foreign sources.

As foreign profits increase, so does foreign employment. The top five U.S. corporations are right ahead of the trend: A large percentage of their workers are based in other countries. Over 50% of Ford Motor Company's employees and 45% of IBM's, for instance, live outside the U.S.

International diversification helps multinationals stay competitive. But it also means that their successes are less likely to benefit U.S. workers. Many corporations are no longer "based" in one country. Someday, they may be like oil tankers, registered for convenience in the country with the least onerous regulations.

Foreign profit of U.S. firms as a percentage of all before-tax profit, 1950-93

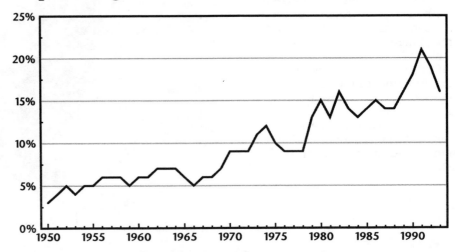

10.11 Worldwide Inequalities

If the world were considered one big country, its income inequality would far surpass that of any actual country in the world today. The relatively affluent countries that belong to the Organization for Economic Cooperation and Development (OECD) comprise 15% of the world population but enjoy 73% of world output. In contrast, the 78% of the population living in developing nations consumes a meager 16% of world output.

Differences in standards of living are so extreme that they are hard to conceptualize: Output per person is about 50 times greater in the U.S. than in China and India. Modern economic development is doing little to close this gap. On the whole, world resources are distributed more unequally today than they were in the 1960s.

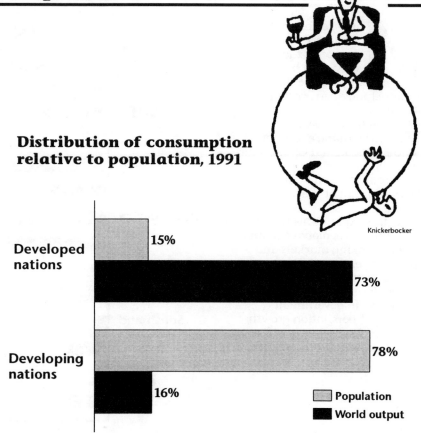

Distribution of consumption relative to population, 1991

Knickerbocker

Developed nations
15%
73%

Developing nations
78%
16%

☐ **Population**
■ **World output**

10.12 Making Progress?

Many regions of the world are in worse economic shape than they were back in 1980. Sub-Saharan Africa was actually better off in 1960 than it is today.

Growth rates have slowed in many areas. With the striking exception of South and East Asia and China, output per capita in developing countries has recently grown at about half the rate of that of the industrialized nations.

Many factors explain this slower rate of growth. Weak global demand has meant shrinking markets and lower prices for exports. Increased debt has led to massive transfers of resources to developed countries and forced cutbacks in government spending. Rapid population growth, particularly in Africa, has made it difficult to raise standards of living.

Knickerbocker

GDP per capita (at 1980 $US and exchange rates)

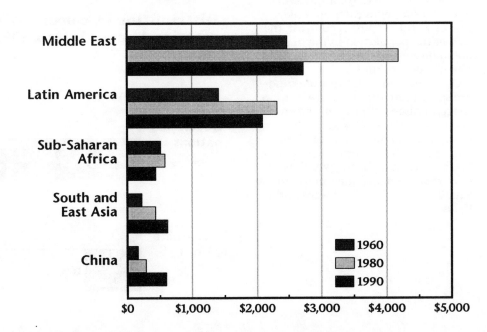

Middle East

Latin America

Sub-Saharan Africa

South and East Asia

China

- ■ 1960
- ▨ 1980
- ■ 1990

$0 $1,000 $2,000 $3,000 $4,000 $5,000

10.13 Does Economic Growth Deliver the Goods?

When it comes to standards of living, GDP per capita is not the name of the game. The distribution of income and public services is even more important.

Sri Lanka, with one-fourth the GDP per capita of Saudi Arabia, outranks that country on quality-of-life indicators such as infant mortality, life expectancy, and literacy rates. Of the school-aged population, 66% can ex-pect to attend secondary schools in Sri Lanka, while only 44% will do so in Saudi Arabia.

Costa Rica and Brazil share similar levels of GDP per capita, but egalitarian public policies have helped Costa Ricans outperform Brazilians on most indicators, including poverty rates among their children. Costa Rica's infant mortality rate is one-quarter of Brazil's. And 12% of all Brazilian children under 5 suffer from some form of malnutrition, compared with 6% in Costa Rica.

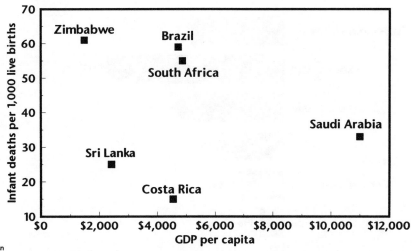

Infant mortality vs. GDP per capita, 1990

Russell Christian

10.14 Crying for Food

The World Food Council estimates that one-fifth of humanity goes to bed hungry every night. Children are the most visibly affected: In South Asia, 59% are underweight. Why? Not for lack of food.

New agricultural technologies (the "green revolution") have been successful in that respect. The real problem is lack of money.

In most developing countries, overall consumption of calories and protein has increased over the last 25 years. But consumption remains far below the level in developed countries. And deficiencies of certain key nutrients, such as vitamin A, iron, and iodine, cause serious health problems for adults as well as children.

Percentage of children underweight, 1990

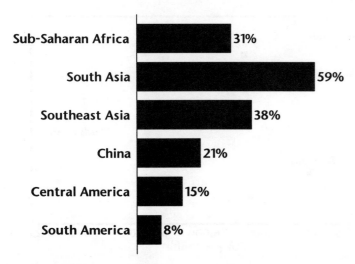

Sub-Saharan Africa	31%
South Asia	59%
Southeast Asia	38%
China	21%
Central America	15%
South America	8%

TODAY'S "INVISIBLE HAND"

DANZIGER
The Christian Science Monitor
Los Angeles Times Syndicate

10.15 Export Dependency

They used to be called "banana republics." While few actually produce bananas, many developing nations are still heavily dependent on a single raw material or an unprocessed agricultural product for their export earnings. This leaves them vulnerable to both the vagaries of world markets and the weather.

Most commodity prices reached a historical high in the mid-1970s, encour- aging many overconfident policy makers in developing countries to borrow heavily against future export earnings. They got into big trouble in the early 1980s, when the prices of primary commodities fell relative to industrial goods, worsening the terms of trade.

Unfortunately, it was mostly ordinary people, not policy makers, who paid the price. Apart from the fact that they could no longer afford to buy needed imports of industrial goods, many suffered the ill effects of cutbacks in government spending and other policies designed to reduce balance-of-payments problems.

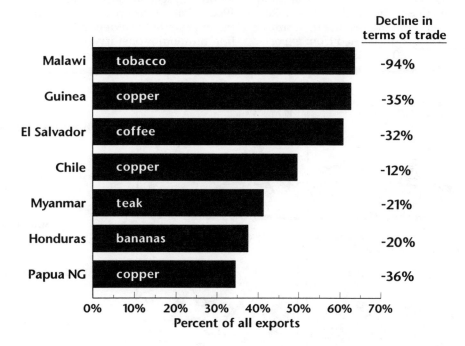

Dominant commodity as a percentage of all merchandise exports, and decline in terms of trade since the mid-1970s

	Dominant commodity	Decline in terms of trade
Malawi	tobacco	-94%
Guinea	copper	-35%
El Salvador	coffee	-32%
Chile	copper	-12%
Myanmar	teak	-21%
Honduras	bananas	-20%
Papua NG	copper	-36%

Percent of all exports

10.16 The Burden of Debt

One and a half trillion dollars is about what developing countries together owe to creditors in other countries. Many are staggering under the burden of debt. Repayment and interest use up a sizable share of dollars earned from exports. Between 1980 and 1990, this situation worsened for all regions of the developing world except Latin America.

Most countries borrowed lots of money in the 1970s, when prospects for growth seemed good. Then, in the 1980s, high interest rates and declining incomes led to a debt crisis. The International Monetary Fund and the World Bank forced many countries to adopt austerity measures in order to qualify for new loans.

During most of the past decade, debt service in developing countries actually exceeded the amount of new loans. So much for aid to development.

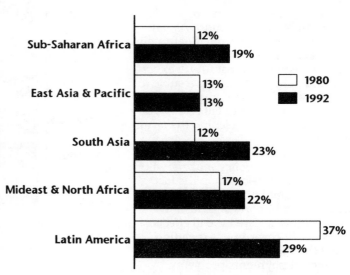

Total debt service as a percentage of exports

	1980	1992
Sub-Saharan Africa	12%	19%
East Asia & Pacific	13%	13%
South Asia	12%	23%
Mideast & North Africa	17%	22%
Latin America	37%	29%

Toolkit

T.1 A GUIDE TO GENERAL SOURCES

This section provides a guide to sources of data and analysis that are useful in economic research. It begins with an overview of general sources, then provides further information for each chapter topic. Use the detailed references in the Sources section of this book to track down or update specific facts and figures.

✦ The two best sources of general economic data are the *Statistical Abstract of the U.S.*, published by the U.S. Bureau of the Census, and *The Economic Report of the President*, published by the President's Council of Economic Advisors. New editions of both normally become available in February from the Government Printing Office (GPO). Catalogs of GPO publications are available from the Superintendent of Documents, Stop SM, Washington, DC 20402.

✦ Short, interesting, and very useful articles about current economic events are published monthly in *Dollars and Sense*, by the Economic Affairs Bureau, Inc., 1 Summer Street, Somerville, MA 02143 (617-628-8411). More academic yet accessible articles are published bi-monthly in *Challenge* (80 Business Park Drive, Armonk, NY 10504).

✦ The major publications of the business press, including *The Wall Street Journal*, *Fortune*, *Forbes*, and *Barron's*, are all useful, but *Business Week* usually offers the most systematic analysis of economic trends. For a distinctly anticorporate approach, see *The Left Business Observer* (250 West 85th Street, New York, NY 10024, 212-874-4020).

✦ For more in-depth reading, *The State of Working America 1994-95* by the Economic Policy Institute offers a comprehensive analysis of the way economic trends affect working Americans.

✦ The Center for Popular Economics provides workshops on economic literacy, international economics, and urban economic issues. Contact us at P. O.Box 785, Amherst, MA 01004 (413-545-0743).

Chapter 1: Owners. Every October for the past several years, *Forbes* magazine has published a feature article describing the richest 400 people in the U.S. in that year. In late spring or early summer, *Fortune* ranks the top industrial corporations of the year and provides considerable information about their performance. In May, *Business Week* usually publishes a list of the highest-paid corporate executives.

For a critical analysis of the impact of money on electoral outcomes, see *Money Talks: Corporate PACs and Political Influence*, by Dan Clawson, Alan Neustadtl, and Denise Scott (New York: Basic Books, 1992).

Chapter 2: Workers. Monthly issues of the Bureau of Labor Statistics' *Employment and Earnings (EE)* are the best source of up-to-date information on labor force participation, industry, occupation, earnings, and unemployment. The January issue provides annual averages for the preceding year. The bureau also publishes *Monthly Labor Review*, which often includes articles on special topics such as displaced workers.

In 1994 the BLS changed some of the definitions it used in its labor force survey. As a result, some figures for 1994 and later years, such as the unemployment rate, are not perfectly comparable with those for earlier years. For more details see "Revisions in the Current Population Survey Effective Jan. 1994," *EE*, Feb. 1994.

Chapter 3: Women. The Bureau of the Census periodically publishes special reports on women. Another useful source of reports and analysis is the Institute for Women's Policy Research (1400 20th St. NW, Suite 104, Washington, D.C. 20036, 202-785-5100). For international comparisons, see *The World's Women, 1970-1990*, published by the United Nations.

Chapter 4: People of Color. The following Bureau of the Census publications provide particularly useful information. *The Black Population in the United States: March 1991* (Current Population Reports, P20-464). *The Hispanic Population in the U.S.: March 1993* (Current Population Reports, P20-475). *We, The First Americans.*

Chapter 5: Government Spending. Every January, the president proposes a budget for the next fiscal year to Congress, detailed in *The Budget of the U.S. Government* and summarized in *The Budget in Brief.*

The best source for historical data on revenue and taxation is *The U.S. Budget, Historical Tables.* These are all annual publications and are available from the Government Printing Office, Washington, D.C. The Center on Budget and Policy Priorities (777 Capital Street NE, Suite 705, Washington, DC 20002, 202-408-1080) publishes regular reports on government spending, particularly as it affects low-income Americans. Citizens for Tax Justice (1311 L Street NW, Washington, DC 20005, 202-626-3780) focuses on tax issues. The National Priorities Project offers critical perspectives on the federal budget (160 Main Sreet, Suite 6, Northampton, MA 01060, 413-584-9556).

Chapter 6: Education and Welfare. In March of every year, the Bureau of the Census conducts a survey of U.S. families to determine trends in income and poverty. The results are published annually in the Current Population Reports (CPR) Series P-60, often under the title *Money Income of Households, Families, and Persons in the United States.* Recently, the Bureau of the Census began to conduct a survey of income and program participation that includes information about who receives public assistance. Some of the results are published in the CPR Series P-70, *Economic Characteristics of Households in the United States.*

Expenditures per recipient in social programs such as Aid to Families with Dependent Children are published monthly by the Social Security Administration in the *Social Security Bulletin*; annual figures are summarized in the January Statistical Supplement. Excellent data, as well as firm advocacy, can be found in the publications of the Children's Defense Fund, including a monthly newsletter and a regular report entitled, *The State of America's Children* (25 E Street NW, Washington, DC 20001, 202-628-8787).

The *Condition of Education* and the *Digest of Educational Statistics*, published by the National Center for Educational Statistics (U.S. Department of Education), are good primary sources on the state of education. For both statistics and articles, see *The Chronicle of Higher Education*, published on a weekly basis.

Chapter 7: Health. Primary sources on the health of Americans are *Health, United States* and *Vital Statistics of the U.S.*, both published annually by the National Center for Health Statistics (U.S. Department of Health and Human Services). Information on health care costs and expenditures can be found in the winter issue of the *Health Care Financing Review* (Office of National Health Statistics), while comparative data on industrial countries is available in the summer issue.

Finally, Physicians for a National Health Program has published a very useful chartbook, *The National Health Program Book: A Source Guide for Advocates* (Monroe, ME: Common Courage Press, 1994).

Chapter 8: Environment. Many different sources are useful here, but an annual publication that provides an overview is the *State of the World*, a research project of the Worldwatch Institute directed by Lester Brown (1776 Massachusetts Avenue NW, Washington, DC 20036, 202-452-1999).

Chapter 9: Macroeconomics. The tables published in the back of *The Economic Report of the President* are an excellent source of summary statistics. Tables in the monthly *Survey of Current Business*, published by the Department of Commerce, and the *Federal Reserve Bulletin*, published by the Board of Governors, Federal Reserve, provide even more current data.

Cross-national macroeconomic data can be found in *Main Economic Indicators*, published by the Organization for Economic Cooperation and Development (OECD), and in *International Financial Statistics* (monthly) and *Balance of Payments Yearbook*, published by the International Monetary Fund (IMF). The Southern Finance Project keeps abreast of developments in the financial sector in the U.S. and publishes regular briefing papers (P. O. Box 334, Philomont, VA 22131, 703-338-7754).

Chapter Ten: The Global Economy. The May issue of the Commerce Department's *Survey of Current Business* summarizes U.S. international transactions for the preceding year. The *Federal Reserve Bulletin* also includes a great deal of data on foreign trade and exchange rates. *U.S. Industrial Outlook*, a yearly publication of the U.S. Department of Commerce, is a good source of information on the international situation of most U.S. industries.

For information on developing countries, the IMF publications mentioned above are good sources for financial data. For comprehensive information on many aspects of economic development, the World Bank in Washington, DC, publishes annually the *World Development Report*, *World Tables*, and *World Debt Tables*, which constitute reliable sources for data .

A more humane approach, oriented toward assessment of human needs, can be found in *The Human Development Report*, an annual publication of the United Nations Development Programme. The United Nations also publishes the annual *World Economic Survey*, which covers major issues facing the world economy, and, every four years, the *Report on the World Social Situation*.

T.2 HOW TO READ AND WRITE GRAPHS

Despite the fact that we are bombarded daily by graphs and graphics, it's easy to be intimidated, confused, or misled by them. The best way to learn to read graphs is to make a few. Once you have a sense of how to make them by hand, you might have the inclination and the opportunity to take advantage of modern software for personal computers that allows you to punch them out with abandon. Here are some basic guidelines for reading graphs:

1. Figure out what the variables are. A graph usually displays a relationship between the values of two or more variables. In bar and line graphs, the value of

one variable is usually represented on a horizontal axis that starts at zero and increases to the right. The values of other variables are usually represented on a vertical axis that starts at zero and increases upward. For instance, look at Chart 2.7: Along the horizontal axis, time increases from 1950 to 1994. Along the vertical axis, the value of earnings runs from 0 to $7.

Pie charts picture the relationship between a whole and its parts, as in Chart 4.1. Columns or bars can be used the same way, as in Chart 4.2.

2. Look at the range of the values of the variables: Sometimes they start, not at zero, but at a higher value, as in Chart 2.5. Often, they are multiples of the numbers indicated, such as thousands or millions. The scale of measurement used largely determines the visual impact of a graph.

3. Ask yourself what you expected the relationship to be. Graphs display patterns. Only a critical, attentive reader can decide whether those patterns really represent important trends.

When you set out to make graphs, follow a similar line of reasoning:

1. Choose the variables whose relationship you want to explore or display; let them determine the type of graph.

2. Decide upon the range and the units you want to use. Experiment with some alternatives, and expect a fair amount of trial and error.

3. Choose the length of your horizontal and vertical axes (or the diameter of your pie). Allow enough space

for the variation you want to show. Note that the relative length of the two axes will determine how the graph looks. Increasing the length of the vertical axis will exaggerate differences in the values; increasing the length of the horizontal axis will minimize them.

A computer can do much of the trial-and-error part of this work, though you still have to make the decisions and enter the numbers. The specifics depend almost entirely on the hardware and software you have access to. In general:

1. You need a computer, a printer, and some kind of graphing software. Though few programs are devoted only to this purpose, many can produce very serviceable graphs. The most versatile are business presentation programs like Freelance Graphics, PowerPoint, Harvard Graphics, and Persuasion. These are designed to combine text, graphs, and illustrations into effective presentations. Spreadsheets (e.g., Lotus123, Excel, Quattro Pr.) will do the job well, and even the new generation of word processors (WordPerfect, Word, AmiPro) have basic graphing capabilities.
2. Most graphing programs allow you to enter data directly. But if you need to process the data at all (e.g., dividing the number of people unemployed by the number of people in the labor force to get the unemployment rate), it's best to put the numbers into a spreadsheet and let it do the figuring for you. Then it's easy to move the results into the graphing program. To produce this book, we created spreadsheets in Lotus123 and imported them to Freelance Graphics, where we made the graphs. Then we pasted the graphs into our page layout program.
3. The software we've been talking about is getting easier and easier to use; it's made for businesspeople, not computer hackers. But the more powerful it is, the longer it takes to learn how to make all its features work for you. So ask for help from somebody who knows how to use it. Read the manual if you have to. Give yourself plenty of time to play around and don't worry about making mistakes. It's only numbers.

T.3 MEANS, MEDIANS, & OTHER MEASURES

Sometimes empirical data is wrapped up in a bewildering variety of statistical terms such as "means" and "medians." You can look up their definition in a dictionary or glossary, but the best way to learn what they mean is to apply them yourself. One way of summarizing information about a large number of cases is to ask what's happening to the "typical" case. For instance, you might want to know the income of the typical U.S. family. There are two common but different ways of estimating this.

The simplest and most common way is to calculate the average, also called the "mean." Take the sum of all family income and divide it by the number of families. Another way to define "typical" is by the median, rather than the mean. Line up all the relevant cases from the lowest value to the highest and choose the one that is closest to the middle: the family whose income was greater than the bottom half but lower than the top half.

Sometimes, the mean and the median are the same. More often, they diverge. The reason is that extreme cases affect the mean more than the median. For instance, if you added one family with an income 100 times greater than the next family, it would pull the average up a great deal but change the median hardly at all. The overall distribution of income, like the distribution of both earnings and wealth, has many more extreme cases on the high side than on the low side. For this reason, the mean over-estimates the income of the typical family, and the median is a better measure.

T.4 REAL VS. NOMINAL: HOW TO USE PRICE INDICES

Most people think that something that is real is just something that is not imaginary. In the economist's world, however, the word "real" describes a number that has been adjusted to take inflation into account. A real value is one that is expressed in constant dollars, or dollars with the same purchasing power. By contrast, a nominal value reflects the value or purchasing power current at the time and is therefore described as being in "current" dollars.

You can use estimates of the rate of inflation to convert nominal values (expressed in current dollars of purchasing power) to real values (expressed in constant dollars of purchasing power). First, you must decide what estimate of the rate of inflation to use. The most commonly used measure is the Consumer Price Index for urban consumers, or CPI-U. This index calculates the number of dollars required to buy a certain "basket of goods" (including food, clothing, and housing) in a certain benchmark year, such as 1967, and determines how many dollars would have been required in another year, such as 1994, to purchase the same basket of goods. The ratio between the two determines the CPI-U.

For instance, in 1993, the CPI-U was 144.5 relative to the benchmark year 1982 = 100. That means that $1.445 in 1993 had the same purchasing power as $1 in 1982 To calculate the value of your 1993 salary of $18,000 in 1982 dollars (and determine if your real wages have increased), set up this formula and plug in the appropriate numbers:

$$\frac{\text{1993 CPI-U}}{\text{1982 CPI-U}} = \frac{\text{Your salary in 1993 dollars}}{\text{Your salary in 1982 dollars}}$$

$$\frac{144.5}{100} = \frac{\$18,000}{x}$$

Using a little algebra ("crossmultiply and divide"—multiply the 1982 CPI-U by the 1993 salary, then divide by the 1993 CPI-U), you can determine that your 1993 earnings have the same purchasing power as $12,456.75 had in 1982.

Suppose you want to compare your real earnings in 1988 with your real earnings in 1993. As long as you can consult an estimate of the CPI-U for the range of years you are interested in, you can use any year as a base year. The 1988 CPI-U is 118.3. You can use the figure you just used for 1993 CPI-U to convert your 1988 salary (say, $18,000 again) to 1988 dollars as follows:

$$\frac{144.5}{118.3} = \frac{\$18,000}{x}$$

A few calculations show that x, your 1993 salary in 1988 dollars, is \$14,736.32. Did you earn more or less than that in 1988?

There are a variety of Consumer Price Indices, and the method used to construct them has changed over time. In particular, the CPI-U developed in 1983 treats housing costs differently (and more appropriately) than the older standard CPI series. The Bureau of Labor Statistics (BLS) has created an adjusted series, the CPI-U-X1, for the years before 1983 that is comparable with the CPI-U.

No index is a perfect measure of the purchasing power of your dollars because the goods and services you spend money on may be different from those included in the basket of goods the BLS uses.

Another complication is that the composition of the average basket of goods people buy varies over time. The rates of price increase vary considerably—in some years, food prices may increase faster; in some years slower than the cost of other commodities. In addition to the Consumer Price Index for all items, the BLS publishes indices for many separate items.

Many important economic data, such as measurements of gross national product or investment, pertain to sums of money that are not really spent by consumers. To convert these sums to real terms, you should use a different index, the Implicit Price Deflator, which is calculated for this purpose. You can use it exactly the same way as the CPI, using either the overall index or an index of one of its separate components.

T.5 THE CENSUS VOCABULARY: FAMILIES, HOUSEHOLDS, PERSONS, AND HEADS

In the language of the Census Bureau, "person" means just what we expect it to—an individual human being. The official bureau terms "families" and "households," however, mean something a little different from their everyday definitions. A family is any group of people related by blood, marriage, or adoption living at the same residence. If you don't live with your parents, you are not considered part of their family (and the census would not consider your income part of their family income). People who live alone are not considered members of families. By official definition, they represent single-person households.

A household consists of all the people living in one residence, whether or not they are related. Individuals, unrelated roommates, and families all qualify; but people living in "institutions" such as prisons, army barracks, and hospitals are not considered part of households. Here's one way to keep the distinction straight: According to the Census Bureau, all families are households, but not all households are families.

People who compile statistics should choose their units of analysis carefully. Sometimes the choice is obvious. You wouldn't want to ask what percentage of households experienced a divorce because many household members aren't even married. On the other hand, you wouldn't want to ask what percentage of families received Social Security because you would be excluding all people living alone, many of whom are elderly.

At other times, the choice is not so obvious. The percentage of all households that include children is arguably just as interesting a "fact" as the percentage of families that include children. But the two percentages mean different things and should not be confused.

Beyond the household/family distinction lies the question of "headship." Until 1980, the bureau always classified a husband as the head of his family if he lived in the same household. A female-headed family household was, by definition, a family household lacking a husband. Now, the census is more diplomatic and designates the person in whose name the home is owned or rented as the householder. If the home is owned or rented jointly by a married couple, either the husband or the wife may be listed first. The families once termed "female-headed" are now termed "families with female householders, no husband present." The Bureau of Labor Statistics has a nicer way of putting it: "families maintained by women."

T.6 WHAT THEY CALL US: RACIAL AND ETHNIC LABELS IN ECONOMIC DATA

Everyone who works with economic statistics about people should pay attention to the implications of racial and ethnic labels. The categories that government agencies such as the Bureau of the Census and the Bureau of Labor Statistics use to define and gather economic data reflect the unspoken assumptions and biases of the larger society. Sometimes, these categories are politically offensive or simply outdated. Sometimes, agencies change and improve the racial and ethnic labels but introduce problems of comparability between data collected in different years. Take, for instance, the category "nonwhite" which government agencies once used to describe African-Americans, Asians, and Native Americans as a group. This category accurately reflects conventional English usage of this period, a usage defined by a white population which automatically considered its own race as the standard. It's a bit like defining women as "nonmen."

The conventional racial categories "white" and "nonwhite" also overlooked the distinctive character and sense of community shared by people whose origins lay in Spanish-speaking countries. In 1979, many government agencies responded to widespread criticism by changing their categories to white, black, and Hispanic (of Spanish origin), providing data for these three groups and largely discontinuing the white/nonwhite distinction. However welcome this change, it made it difficult to construct long-run data series. There is no data predating 1979 for blacks and Hispanics as separate groups, and there is very little data after 1978 for Asians, Native Americans, or people of color as a whole.

The 1990s have witnessed more change and controversy. Many blacks (though not all), preferring to be described according to ethnic heritage, now choose to be called "African-Americans." The term "Hispanic" has been criticized because it misleadingly implies Spanish origin. Perhaps the greatest failing of official terminology is the lack of a "multiracial" category, even though much of the population actually has a mixed heritage.

It is easy to overlook the implications of racial/ethnic distinctions. For instance, you might think that you could arrive at the total number of families in poverty by adding together white families in poverty, African-American families in poverty, and Latino families in poverty. Not so. Latino is an ethnic, not a racial designation. Latinos can be categorized either as black or white; if you add their numbers to the numbers of black and white families, you will overcount the total. At the same time, you will overlook those Asian and Native American families that live in poverty.

For the most part, the Census Bureau invites people to define their own race and ethnicity, and there are no hard-and-fast rules for people to follow. For instance, American Indians became more assertive of their cultural pride and political rights in the 1970s, and many people who had never done so before identified themselves as Indians. If you didn't know this, you might infer incorrectly from census publications that American Indians had an extraordinarily high rate of population growth.

Because racial categories change, it is sometimes difficult to follow one series of data over a long period of time. For instance, until 1978 the Handbook of Labor Statistics provided data on average earnings for "Black and other" workers. Beginning in 1979, the category changed to "Black." One might be tempted to splice the two series together. But this would be misleading; "Black and other" included people of Asian origin, whose relatively high incomes raised the average earnings of the group significantly above those of African-Americans.

No matter how careful you are, you still have to make difficult decisions about how to categorize different groups of people. In this book, we depend upon the racial and ethnic categories used by the government agencies that collect statistical data but sometimes use a different nomenclature. We prefer "African-American" to "black," and "Latino" to "Hispanic," though we occasionally use all four terms. We provide more disaggregated data wherever feasible.

Because we think there is an important political and cultural boundary between whites and a group that includes African-Americans, Latinos, Asians, and Native Americans, we use the term "people of color" as an alternative to "nonwhite." It is an alternative, not a synonym, because it includes Latinos, which "nonwhite" does not. We use the term "Native Americans" to refer to the group the Bureau of the Census labels "American Indians, Eskimos, and Aleuts."

T.7 MEASURING GROWTH: WHAT'S GROSS ABOUT GROSS DOMESTIC PRODUCT?

When economists use the word "gross," they usually mean "total." Gross domestic product (GDP) is simply the total value of all the goods and services produced for sale within a country (usually in a given year). But there is something a little gross, even downright vulgar, about using GDP as a measure of total production or economic welfare. None of the many goods and services produced in households are included in GDP because they aren't sold. And GDP doesn't reflect changes in the quantity or quality of goods that don't have a price tag, such as clean air or good health. But unless and until a better summary of production is widely adopted, GDP will remain central to the national income accounts that government agencies use to track the growth of the economy over time.

Until recently, the Bureau of Economic Analysis emphasized the gross national product (GNP), or the value of all goods and services produced by U.S. firms or U.S. citizens (whether inside or outside the country). In 1991, it began to use GDP for two reasons: first, to make U.S. national accounting figures compatible with those of other countries, and, second, because the GDP, in contrast with the GNP, emphasizes production located in the United States, no matter who gets the income from it. In other words, income earned by foreigners on economic activities taking place in the U.S. is included in the GDP, while it is not in the GNP. Similarly, income earned by Americans on investment in foreign countries is not included in the GDP but is a component of the GNP. As the U.S. is getting more and more integrated into the global economy, the GDP gives a more reliable picture of economic activity taking place in the U.S.

The national accounts break GDP down into four components:

1. Goods and services purchased by households and individuals, or personal consumption expenditures.
2. Those purchased by businesses, or gross private domestic investment, including investment in inventory.
3. Exports minus imports, or net exports (negative in recent years).
4. Government purchases.

Estimates of the value of these items in the national accounts are usually released quarterly by the Bureau of Economic Analysis, often seasonally adjusted and converted to an annual rate in order to make them more easily comparable. A detailed explanation of the national accounts system is provided in *The U.S. Economy Demystified: What the Major Economic Statistics Mean and Their Significance for Business*, by Albert T. Sommers (Lexington, MA: D.C. Heath and Company, 1985).

T.8 UPPERS AND DOWNERS: THE BUSINESS CYCLE

Economic growth fluctuates, and its ups and downs are usually described as part of a cycle of recession and recovery. Economists declare a recession when GNP declines (in other words, when economic growth is negative) for 2 quarters of a year in a row. A recession year is one in which GNP is lower than it was in the previous year. "Depression" is a word reserved for deep, dark recessions that last a long time. There is no technical definition for a recovery; but the term usually refers to the period immediately after recession, when growth is restored.

Why is the economy plagued by a business cycle? At least a dozen explanations have been offered, including one that blames sunspots. But most economists agree that the business cycle is closely related to fluctuations in the level of business investment. That level is determined by expected costs and expected profits, which shift in both predictable and unpredictable ways.

Because the business cycle has such an important impact on virtually all economic indicators, it's important to keep it in mind when interpreting economic statistics and to distinguish between short-run and long-run trends. Imagine, for instance, a beach at the ocean. If the water is calm and there are no waves, it's easy to tell whether the tide is moving in or out. But a lot of waves can disguise the movement of the tide. To see which way it's going, you might need to compare the distance from peak to peak (or from trough to trough) of several succeeding waves. Economists use the word "secular" to describe trends that are not cyclical.

T.9 A GUIDE TO THE FEDERAL BUDGET

Every January, the president presents a proposed budget for the next fiscal year (FY) to Congress. For example, in January 1993, President Clinton transmitted his budget for fiscal year 1994, which runs from October 1, 1993, to September 30, 1994. This budget presents the administration's proposals for all the different programs of the federal government, including national defense, Social Security, Medicaid, and education. It explains and defends the spending required to meet the administration's objectives in all these areas. It also projects government revenues for the fiscal year and, consequently, the federal deficit.

The president's budget is only a proposal until it is passed by Congress and signed into law by the president. Congressional work on the budget originates in the spring in the House of Representatives. After lengthy work by the House Appropriations Committee, the House votes on an appropriations bill. The approved budget proposal is sent to the Senate, which comes up with its own version. A House and Senate conference committee then works out the differences between the two proposals, and the final bill is sent to the president. The president then has the choice of either signing the bill into law or vetoing it, but he cannot amend it.

The federal budget process has a terminology (as well as a logic) of its own. For instance, there is an important difference between budget authority and outlays. The term "budget authority" describes an amount of money that is authorized for a particular program, which might last for several years. "Outlays" refers to the amount of money spent out of the budget authority "checking account" during a particular fiscal year. When calculating the budget deficit, one must focus on budget outlays. Budget authorities often extend over several budget years; in a given fiscal year, most federal spending is in a sense predetermined by previous budgets. Given the existence of both budget authority and entitlements (such as Social Security, veterans' benefits, and Medicare), only a small component of the federal budget is discretionary in a given budget year.

Economists disagree over the correct definition of the federal deficit. One issue is a component of the budget known as the Social Security Trust Fund, money accumulated to help pay future Social Security claims. This fund currently has a large surplus, which makes the deficit look much smaller. But since it is money that must be spent at some future date, Congress decided it should not be included. The Omnibus Budget Reconciliation Act of 1990 enshrined Social Security as an "off-budget" item, which means it is not counted when calculating the deficit.

For a good discussion of this and other issues surrounding the definition of the deficit, see Robert Eisner, *The Misunderstood Economy: What Counts and How to Count It* (Boston: Harvard Business School Press, 1994).

T.10 POVERTY AND THE POVERTY LINE

Feeling poor in the U.S. is not the same thing as officially being poor. The U.S. government includes a person or family among the poor if their income falls below an officially designated poverty line or "threshold" that varies according to family size.

In 1992, the poverty threshold for a single person was $7,143; for a family of 4 including 2 children, it was $14,228. Every year, these thresholds are adjusted for inflation.

This definition of poverty is problematic for a number of reasons. First, the original threshold was set in a somewhat arbitrary way that has become increasingly inaccurate over time. Second, it is misleading to define poverty entirely in absolute, rather than in relative, terms. In 1960, the poverty line for a family of 4 amounted to about 54% of median family income; but by 1992, it had fallen to about 35%. In relative terms, poor families were much poorer in 1992.

These are good reasons to raise the poverty line, but of course, doing so would increase the poverty rate (the percentage of people with incomes below the poverty line). Revisions that would decrease the official poverty rate have received far more recent attention.

Since the mid-1970s, government transfer programs have provided large amounts of noncash or in-kind assistance, such as food stamps, Medicaid, and subsidized housing. It's difficult to estimate the "market value" of such benefits. For instance, if the value of services received through Medicaid were counted as if it were cash income, a person could escape official poverty simply by getting very sick. Still, the failure to include some estimate of noncash transfers in calculations of family income biases the official poverty rate upward. This compensates to some extent for the effect of setting the poverty line very low.

Changes in the definition of the poverty line affect calculations of trends as well as levels of poverty. If the full value of noncash transfers is included in calculations of family income in the 1980s and no other revisions are made, estimates of the poverty rate are lower. However, the estimated increase in the poverty rate between 1980 and 1992 is even greater because cuts in social spending diminished the relative size of noncash transfers to poor people.

For a good discussion of these issues, see Patricia Ruggles, *Drawing the Line: Alternative Poverty Measures and Their Implications for Public Policy* (Washington, DC: The Urban Institute Press, 1990).

Sources

For a general guide to sources, see T.1. This list uses the following abbreviations:

BC   U.S. Bureau of the Census
BLS   U.S. Bureau of Labor Statistics
BS   *Balance Sheets for the U.S. Economy*, Board of Governors, Federal Reserve System
BW   *Business Week* (weekly)
CPR   *Current Population Report*, BC (semimonthly)
CSM   *Christian Science Monitor*
DHHS   U.S. Department of Health and Human Services
DS   *Dollars and Sense* (monthly)
EE   *Employment and Earnings*, U.S. Dept. of Labor
EPI   Economic Policy Institute, Washington, DC
ERP   *Economic Report of the President*, President's Council of Economic Advisors (annual)
FRB   *Federal Reserve Bulletin*, Board of Governors, Federal Reserve System (monthly)
GAO   General Accounting Office, Washington, DC
GPO   Government Printing Office, Washington, DC
HCFR   *Health Care Financing Review*
HLS   *Handbook of Labor Statistics*, U.S. Dept. of Labor
HT   *Historical Tables*, Budget of U.S. Government
LAT   *Los Angeles Times* (daily)
MLR   *Monthly Labor Review*, BLS (monthly)
NEA   National Education Association
NHPB   David Himmelstein and Steffie Woolhandler, *The National Health Program Book: A Source Guide for Advocates* (Monroe, ME: Common Courage Press, 1994)
NIPA   *National Income and Product Accounts*, U.S. Department of Commerce, Bureau of Economic Analysis
NYT   *New York Times* (daily)
OECD   Organization for Economic Cooperation and Development
OMB   Office of Management and Budget
SA   *Statistical Abstract of the U.S.*, BC (annual)
SCB   *Survey of Current Business*, U.S. Dept. of Commerce
SWA   Lawrence Mishel and Jared Bernstein, *The State of Working America*, EPI Series (Armonk, NY: M.E. Sharpe, annual)
UN   United Nations
WDR   *World Development Report*, World Bank (New York: Oxford University Press, 1992)
WP   *Washington Post* (daily)
WSJ   *Wall Street Journal* (daily, except weekends)

Chapter 1: Owners

1.1   Survey of Income and Program Participation, *Household Wealth and Asset Ownership: 1991* (BC, P-70, no. 34) p. vii, Table B.

1.2   Sylvia Nasar, "Fed Gives New Evidence of 80s Gains by Richest, *NYT*, 4/2/92, p. A-1. Sylvia Nasar, "The 1980s: A Very Good Time for the Very Rich, *NYT*, 3/5/92, p. A-1. Jason DeParle, "Bad Year, Good Decade for the Rich," *NYT*, 12/20/91, p. A-16. See also Arthur Kennickell and Janice Shack-Marquez, "Changes in Family Finances from 1983 to 1989: Evidence from the Survey of Consumer Finances," *FRB* 78, no. 1 (Jan. 1992), pp. 1-18.

1.3 *Money Income of Households, Families, and Persons in the U.S.: 1992* (CPR, P-60, # 184), p. 174, Table 34.

1.4 Arthur B. Kennickell and R. Louise Woodburn, "Estimation of Household Net Worth Using Model-Based and Design-Based Weights: Evidence from the 1989 Survey of Consumer Finances," Apr. 1992, (available from the first author at Board of Governors, Federal Reserve, Mail Stop 180, Washington, DC 20551) Table 1. "Changes in Family Finances from 1983 to 1989: Evidence from the Survey of Consumer Finances," *FRB* 78 no. 1 (Jan. 1992), p. 5.

1.5 "The Billionaires," *Fortune*, 6/28/93, p. 44.

1.6 "Executive Pay: The Party Ain't Over Yet," *BW*, 4/26/93, pp. 56-62.

1.7 Dan Clawson, *Money Talks* (New York: Basic Books, 1992), p. 12.

1.8 Dan Clawson and Alan Neustadtl, "Corporate Hegemony, Soft Money and Campaign Finance Reform," Dept. of Sociology, University of Massachusetts, Amherst, MA 01003, p. 19, Table 1.

1.9 William G. Shepherd, personal communication. Background: W.G. Shepherd, *The Economics of Industrial Organization*, 3d ed. (Englewood Cliffs, NJ: Prentice-Hall, 1990). Larry L. Deutsch, ed., *Industry Studies* (Englewood Cliffs, N.J.: Prentice-Hall, 1993).

1.10 *Fortune*, annual feature, "The Largest U.S. Industrial Corporations," July 1962, pp. 172-78; 5/8/78, pp. 240-50; 5/18/94, p. 220. *BS 1945-93*, pp. 32-37, Table B-104. Note: a table of the same name in the first edition of this book was incorrect. It used the wrong measure for the total assets of nonfinancial corporations (which appears in the denominator of the ratio) and therefore overstated the share of assets owned by the top 100 industrial firms.

1.11 John Greenwald, "The Large Economy Size," *Time*, 7/15/91, p. 48. Gary Hector, "Do Bank Mergers Make Sense?" *Fortune*, 8/12/91, p. 70.

1.12 *WDR*, p. 222. *Fortune*, 7/26/93, p. 191.

1.13 National Center for Employee Ownership, press release. "Net Growth of Employee Stock Ownership, 1975-92." *Employee Ownership Report* 14, no. 3 (May-June 1994), p. 1. *ERP 1994*, p. 306, Table B-33. Note: According to NCEO, the number of ESOP participants is difficult to determine. The 1994 figure is their best estimate.

1.14 Joseph Piacentini, *Databook on Employee Benefits* (Washington: Employee Benefit Research Institute, 1992), p. 150, Table 4.18. *ERP 1994*, p. 398, Table B-114. *ERP 1994*, p. 272, Table B-3. Text: "The Politics of Pension Investments," *Labor Economic Notes* (Nov.-Dec. 1992) pp. 2-7. *BW*, 8/9/93, pp. 64-65.

Chapter 2: Workers

2.1 *ERP 1995*, p. 317, Table B-37.

2.2 *EE* 40, no. 1 (Jan. 1993), p. 85, Table B-1. *ERP 1993*, p. 382, Table B-30.

2.3 *SWA 1994-95*, p. 154, Table 3.28. Text: Robert M. Costrell, "Industrial Employment Shift and Wage Growth, 1948-87," a study prepared for the Joint Economic Committee, Washington, August 1988.

2.4 Polly Callaghan and Heidi Hartmann, "Contingent Work" (EPI, 1991). Text: Chris Tilly, "Reasons for the Continuing Growth of Part-Time Employment," *MLR* (Mar. 1991), pp. 10-18.

2.5 BLS, *Employment, Hours, and Earnings*, 1909-84, vol. 2 (Bulletin 1312-12). *EE* 41, no. 1 (Jan. 1994), p. 131,

Table C-1. *EE* 41, no. 10 (Oct. 1994), p. 65, Table B-11. Note: 1994 based on Jan.-Sept. average. 1994 data are not perfectly comparable to earlier years. See *Toolkit* T.1.

2.6 *HLS 1980* (Bulletin 2070), p. 118, Table 60. *HLS 1985* (Bulletin 2217), p. 94, Table 41. *EE*, January issues, 1985-94, Table 54. *EE* 41, no. 10 (Oct. 1994), p. 152, Table D-19. *ERP 1994*, p. 338, Table B-61. Note: before 1979, no data were collected specifically for Latinos. 1994 based on third quarter. Data for 1994 are not perfectly comparable; see *Toolkit* T.1.

2.7 *SA 1993*, p. 429, Table 675. *ERP 1994*, p. 338, Table B-61. *CPI Detailed Report*, Sept. 1994, p. 2, Table Q-3. Note: CPI-U for 1994 derived from seasonally adjusted annual rate for 9 months ended Sept. 1994.

2.8 BLS, press release, 9/30/94, Tables 3 and 5.

2.9 *SWA 1994-95*, p. 126, Table 3.10. Text: *SWA 1994-95*, p. 130, Table 3.12; p. 131, Table 3.13.

2.10 *SWA 1994-95*, p. 147, Table 3.23. Text: Julie Lopez, "College Class of '93 Learns Hard Lesson," *WSJ* 5/20/93, p. B-10.

2.11 *EE* 41, no. 10 (Oct. 1994), p. 18, Table A-9; p. 19, Table A-10. Note: Rates are based on Jan.-Sept. average.

2.12 *ERP 1995*, p. 320, Table B-40. Data for 1994 are not perfectly comparable; see *Toolkit* T.1.

2.13 GAO, "Dislocated Workers, Worker Adjustment and Retraining Notification Act Not Meeting Its Goals," Report to Congressional Committees, Feb. 1993, pp. 12, 22, 24.

2.14 *MLR*, Sept. 1994, pp. 118-19, Table 46-47. *MLR*, June 1987, p. 104, Table 46.

2.15 Figures for 1950-1978 from *HLS 1980*, p. 412, Table 165, converted to percentage of all employees using *ERP 1993*, p. 382, Table B-30. Figures for 1979, 1981, and 1982 interpolated. Figure for 1980 from Larry T. Adams, "Changing Employment Patterns of Organized Workers," *MLR* (Feb. 1985), p. 26. *EE* 32, no. 1 (Jan. 1985), p. 208, Table 32. *EE* 34, no. 1 (Jan. 1987), p. 219, Table 59. *EE* 36, no. 1 (Jan. 1989), p. 225, Table 59. *EE* 39, no. 1 (Jan. 1992), p. 228, Table 57. *EE* 40, no. 1 (Jan. 1993), p. 238, Table 57. *EE* 41, no. 1 (Jan. 1994), p. 248, Table 57.

2.16 *EE* 41, no. 1 (Jan. 1994), pp. 248-49, Tables 57 and 58.

Chapter 3: Women

3.1 *Employment and Training Report of the President, 1982*, pp. 155-57, Table A-5. *EE* (Jan. 1984-94) Tables 3 and 4. BLS, "Labor Force Statistics Derived from the Current Population Survey: A Databook," vol. 1, Bulletin 2096 (Sept. 1982), p. 716, Table C-11. *SA 1986*, p. 399, Table 675. *SA 1994*, p. 402, Table 626.

3.2 Beth Ann Shelton, *Women, Men, and Time: Gender Differences in Paid Work, Housework, and Leisure* (Westport, CT : Greenwood Press, 1992), pp 66-68.

3.3 1970 *U.S. Census*, U.S. Summary, sec. 2, pp. 718-24, Table 21. 1980 *U.S. Census*, pt. 1-A, pp. 166-75, Table 276. *EE* 38, no. 1 (Jan. 1991), p. 37, Table A-22. *EE* 41, no. 1 (Jan. 1994), p. 35, Table A-22.

3.4 Unpublished data, *Current Population Survey*, BLS.

3.5 *Money Income of Households, Families, and Persons in the U.S. 1992* (CPR, P-60, no. 184) p. B-37, Table B-18.

3.6 Unpublished data from *Current Population Survey*, BLS. Text: "State Farm to Pay Women $157 Million for Job Bias," *LAT*, 4/29/92, p. A-1. Jane Gross, "Big Grocery Chain Reaches Landmark Sex-Bias Accord," *NYT*, 10/17/93, p. A-1

3.7 *EE* 40, no. 1 (Jan. 1993), p. 231, Table 54. International Labour Office, Geneva, *Yearbook of Labour Statistics 1992*, pp. 802-04, Table 16.

3.8 Unpublished data from *Current Population Survey*, BLS. Paula England, "Work for Pay and Work at Home: Women's Double Disadvantage," in Craig Calhoun and George Ritzer, eds., *Social Problems* (New York: McGraw Hill, 1993). Text: News Release, 5/20/93, Institute for Women's Policy Research, 1400 20th St. NW, Suite 104, Washington, DC 20036.

3.9 *SA 1986*, p. 39, Table 54. *SA 1994*, p. 58, Table 66. Text: *SA 1994*, p. 58, Table 65. *SA 1994*, p. 59, Table 67.

3.10 *SA 1985*, p. 46, Table 46. Text: *SA 1994*, p. 65, Table 77.

3.11 *SA 1993*, p. 385, Table 611. Andrea Beller and John Graham, *Small Change: The Economics of Child Support* (New Haven: Yale University Press, 1993), p. 36. Spencer Rich, "Children Feel Financial Pinch When Families Split," *WP*, 3/7/91, A-21. "Child Support Money Is Up but Far Short," NYT, 1/7/94, A-14.

3.12 Women's Action Coalition, *The Facts About Women* (New York: The New Press, 1993), pp. 7, 8, 25. *SA 1992*, p. 74, Table 100.

3.13 *Characteristics of the Population Below the Poverty Level: 1976* (CPR, P-60, no. 115), cover. *Poverty in the U.S., 1992* (CPR, P-60, no. 185), p. 1, Table 1. Text: *SA 1994*, p. 476, Table 729.

3.14 Teresa Amott, "The War on Welfare: Clinton's Carrots and Sticks," *DS* (Nov./Dec. 1993) pp. 14-15.

3.15 *SA 1993*, p. 384, Table 610. Text: "Parents' Heavy Burden of Child-Care Costs," *WSJ*, 1/7/92, p. B-8. "Child's Play," *WSJ*, 7/7/93, A-1

3.16 Susan Chira, "Family Leave Is Law: Will Things Change?" *NYT*, 8/15/93, p. E-3. National Commission on Children, *Beyond Rhetoric. A New American Agenda for Children and Families* (Washington: GPO, 1991), p. 84. Steven Greenhouse, "If the French Can Do It, Why Can't We?" *NYT Magazine*, 11/14/93, p. 59. Sheila Kamerman and Alfred Kahn, eds., *Child Care, Parental Leave and the Under 3s: Policy Innovation in Europe* (New York: Auburn House, 1991).

Chapter 4: People of Color

4.1 *SA 1994*, p. 18; Table 18.

4.2 *SA 1993*, p. 18, Table 18.

4.3 *SA 1993*, p. 18, Table 18. Text—*SA 1993*, p. 48, Tables 51 and 52; p. 471, Table 741.

4.4 *Hispanic Americans Today* (*CPR*, P-23, no. 183, 1993) p. 15, Fig. 20. Text: Rebecca L. Clark and Jeffrey S. Passel, "Studies Are Deceptive," *NYT*, 3/9/93, p. A-23. "Immigrants and Income," *WP*, 5/25/94, p. A-28.

4.5 *SA 1987*, p 436, Table 732. *SA 1993*, p. 469, Table 715. *ERP 1994*, p. 338, Table B-61. Text: T. J. Eller, *Household Wealth and Asset Ownership, 1991* (*CPR*, *Survey of Income and Program Participation*, P-70, no. 34). *Money Income of Households, Families, and Persons in the U.S.: 1991* (*CPR*, P-60, no. 180), p. 11, Table 6.

4.6 *SA 1993*, p. 469, Table 735. *SA 1994*, p. 475, Table 727. Text: *SA 1994*, p. 475, Table 728.

4.7 *HLS*, Bulletin 2217, pp. 69-73, Table 27. *EE* (Jan. issues, 1986-94) Table A-63. *EE* 41, no. 10 (Oct. 1994), p. 13, Table A-4; p. 19, Table A-10. Note: 1994 figures based on Jan.-Sept. average.

4.8 *EE* 41, no. 1 (Jan. 1994), p. 22, Table A-7.

4.9 *EE* 41, no. 1 (Jan. 1994), p. 69, Table A-60; p. 81, Table A-75.

4.10 *SA 1993*, p. 318, Table 501; p. 395, Table 625.

4.11 *SA 1984*, p. 434, Table 716. *EE* 40, no. 1 (Jan. 1993), p. 79, Table A-73.

4.12 *SWA 1992-93*, p. 191.

4.13 Richard Verdugo, "Earnings Differentials Between Black, Mexican-American and Non-Hispanic White Male Workers: On the Cost of Being a Minority Worker, 1972-1987," *Social Science Quarterly* 73, no. 3 (Sept. 1992), pp. 663-74. Genevieve Kenney and Douglas Wissoker, "An Analysis of the Correlates of Discrimination Facing Young Hispanic Job-Seekers," *American Economic Review* 84, no. 3 (June 1994), pp. 674-83. David Wessel, "Racial Bias Against Black Job Seekers Remains Pervasive, Broad Study Finds," *WSJ*, 5/15/91, p. A-8. Stephen Labaton, "Dennys Gets a Bill for the Side Order of Bigotry," *NYT*, 5/29/94, p. D-4.

4.14 *SA 1993*, p. 157, Table 232.

4.15 *SA 1993*, p. 61, Table 74.

4.16 *SA 1994*, p. 62, Table 71.

4.17 Douglas Massey and Nancy Denton, *American Apartheid. Segregation and the Making of the Underclass* (Cambridge: Harvard University Press, 1993), p. 224.

4.18 Jim Campen, "Hard Proof That Banks Discriminate," *DS* 191 (Jan./Feb. 1994), pp. 16-19, 36.

Chapter 5: Government Spending

5.1 *ERP 1994*, p. 359, Table B-77. Note: figures for 1994 and 1995 based on estimates.

5.2 *HT 1994*, pp. 21-22, Table 2.1; pp. 35-41, Table 3.1. *ERP 1994*, p. 268, Table B-1; p. 398, Table B-114.

5.3 *OECD Economic Outlook 55* (June 1994), p. A-29; Annex Table 26.

5.4 OECD *Economic Outlook 53* (June 1993), p. 38, Table 9.

5.5 Dean Baker, "Rapid Deficit Reduction: The Fast Path to Slow Growth," EPI Briefing Paper, Aug. 1993.

5.6 *HT 1994*, pp. 39-41, Table 3.1.

5.7 *SA 1994* pp. 334-35, Table 509.

5.8 *HT 1994*, pp. 36-42, Table 3.1; p. 122, Table 9.1; p. 140, Table 10.1.

5.9 National Priorities Project, *In Search of Security. Reducing America's Military, Rebuilding America's Communities* (Northampton, MA, 1994), p. 1.

5.10 James Cypher, "The War Dividend," *DS* 166 (May 1991), p. 9. David Evans, "Wounded Defense Industry Sets Its Sights Abroad," *Business and Society Review* 88 (Winter 1994), pp. 13-18.

5.11 *HT 1995*, pp. 23-24, Table 2.2. Figures for 1995 are estimates.

5.12 *HT 1995*, pp. 21-22, Table 2.1. *ERP 1991*, p. 387, Table B-87. *ERP 1995* p. 379, Table B-90. Note: Profits for 1994 based on average of first 3 quarters. 1994 taxes are estimated

5.13 Wallace C. Peterson, *Silent Depression: The Fate of the American Dream* (New York: W. W. Norton, 1994), p. 105. Text: Citizens for Tax Justice, *Inequality and the Federal Budget Deficit* (Washington, 1991), p. 8. *SA 1993*, p. 332, Table 514.

5.14 *SWA 1994-95*, p. 106, Table 2.14. Text: Citizens for Tax Justice, *A Far Cry from Fair* (Washington, 1991), p. 18.

5.15 Center for Responsive Politics (Washington, 1994).

5.16 Peter G. Petersen, *Facing Up* (New York: Simon and Schuster, 1993), Chart 4.14.

Chapter 6: Education and Welfare

6.1 *Money Income of Households, Families, and Persons in the U.S. 1992 (CPR,* P-60, no. 184), p. B-24, Table B-11.

6.2 *Money Income of Households, Families, and Persons in the U.S.. 1992 (CPR,* P-60, no. 184), pp. B6-7, Table B-3. Text: "Inequality Hurts," *BW,* 8/15/94, pp. 78-84. Louis S. Richman, "The Truth About the Rich and the Poor," *Fortune,* 9/21/92, pp. 134-46.

6.3 *Poverty in the U.S., 1992 (CPR,* P-60, no. 185), pp. 2-3, Table 2.

6.4 *Poverty in the U.S., 1992 (CPR,* P-60 no. 185), p. 6, Table 4; p. xi, Table B. Text: "In Debate on U.S. Poverty, Two Studies Fuel the Argument on Who Is to Blame," *NYT,* 10/29/91, p. A-20.

6.5 *Poverty in the U.S., 1992 (CPR.* P-60, no. 185), p. A-6, Table A-2. Trudi Renwick and Barbara Bergmann, "A Budget-based Definition of Poverty, With an Application to Single-parent Families," *Journal of Human Resources* 28, no. 1 (Winter 1993), pp. 1-24. Patricia Ruggles, *Drawing the Line* (Washington: Urban Institute Press, 1990).

6.6 *Poverty in the U.S., 1992 (CPR,* P-60, no. 185), p. 4, Table 3. Text: see Chart 6.9.

6.7 Michael Wines, "Taxpayers Are Angry. They're Expensive Too." *NYT,* 11/20/94, p. E-5. Steven Waldman, "Benefits 'R' Us," *Newsweek,* 8/10/92, p. 56. Tom Kennedy, "Natural Resource Users Facing Cuts in Subsidies," *WP,* 2/18/93, p. A-4

6.8 *Poverty in the U.S., 1992* (CPR, P-60, no. 185), p. 32, Table 7. Text: Greg Duncan, *Years of Poverty, Years of Plenty* (Ann Arbor: University of Michigan Institute for Social Research, 1984), p. 77.

6.9 *Social Security Bulletin, Annual Statistical Supplement 1992,* p. 319. *Poverty in the U.S. 1990 (CPR.* P-60, no. 175), p. 195. *ERP 1993,* p. 414, Table B-58.

6.10 "The Economic Crisis of Urban America," *BW,* 5/18/92, p. 40. *Poverty in the U.S., 1992,* (CPR, P-60 no. 185) p. 145, Table 22. *ERP 1992,* p. 348, Table B-1; p. 382, Table B-30; p. 437, Table B-75. Paul Taylor, "Children in Poverty: Who Are They?" *WP,* 6/3/91, p. A-7.

6.11 *Housing in America: 1989/90 (BC, Current Housing Reports,* H-123, no. 91-1), pp. 22, 24. John Devaney, BC, personal communication, 12/30/93.

6.12 Center on Budget and Policy Priorities, Washington, *The States and the Poor. How Budget Decisions in 1991 Affected Low Income People,* pp. 46, 49. "The Invisible Parade," *NYT,* 2/20/94, p. E-12.

6.13 *SA 1994* p. 168, Table 251.

6.14 Jonathan Walters, "School Funding," *The Congressional Quarterly Researcher,* 8/27/93, pp. 747-51.

6.15 *SA 1980,* p. 451, Table 745. *SA 1994,* p. 469, Table 715. NEA, *Digest of Education Statistics 1993,* pp. 308-09, Table 306. Text: William Honan, "Cost of a 4-Year Degree Passes $100,000 Mark," *NYT,* 5/4/94, p. B-9.

6.16 U.S. Department of Education, *The Condition of Education* (1993), p. 396, Table 52.2. *HT 1994,* p. 162-73, Table 11.3. *ERP 1993,* p. 376, Table B-24; p. 381, Table B-29. Text: William Honan, "Cost of a 4-Year Degree Passes $100,000 Mark," *NYT,* 5/4/94, p. B-9. "What About Needy Students?" *WP,* 5/11/93, p. A-18.

Chapter 7: Health

7.1 DHHS, *Health USA,* Tables 18 and 114.

7.2 Cathy Cowan and Patricia McDonnell, "Business, Households, and Governments: Health Spending, 1991," *HCFR* 14, no. 3 (Spring 1993), p. 228. Note:

Does not include nonpatient revenue.

7.3 *SA 1975*, p. 423, Table 688. *SA 1986*, p. 478, Table 797. *SA 1994*, p. 489, Table 748.

7.4 *SA 1994*, pp. 127-28, Tables 181, 182, 185. Text: *WSJ*, 4/5/90, p. B-1; 6/6/90, p. A-1. *NHPB*, p. 126.

7.5 *Fortune*, annual "Fortune 500" issues, 1962-1994 (usually published in early April). Text: *Fortune*, 7/29/91, p. 52. Special Committee on Aging, U.S. Senate, *Prescription Drug Prices: Are We Getting Our Money's Worth?* (August 1989), pp. 5-7, 28.

7.6 Roger A. Reynolds and Robert L. Ohsfeldt, eds., *Socioeconomic Characteristics of Medical Practice* (Chicago: American Medical Association, Center for Health Policy Research, 1984), p. 113 ,Table 41. Martin Gonzalez, ed., *Socioeconomic Characteristics of Medical Practice* (Chicago: AMA, Center for Health Policy Research, 1993), p. 150, Table 53. *HLS 1980* (Bulletin 2070) p. 118, Table 60. *HLS 1985* (Bulletin 2217), p. 94, Table 41. *EE*, January issues, 1985-93, Table 54. *ERP 1993*, p. 414, Table B-58. Text: *OECD Health Systems, Facts and Trends 1960-1991* (1993), p. 171, Table 5.1.2; p. 173, Table 5.1.4.

7.7 *Canadian Health Insurance: Lessons for the U.S.* (Washington: GAO, 1991), p. 31. Suzanne Letsch, Helen Lazenby, Katharine Levit, and Cathy Cowan, "National Health Expenditures, 1991," *HCFR* 14, no. 2 (Winter 1992), pp. 1-30. *NHPB*, pp. 127-28. Text: Sally Burner, Daniel Waldo, and David McKusick, "National Health Care Expenditures Projections Through 2030," *HCFR* 14, no. 1 (Fall 1992), p. 15.

7.8 DHHS, *Health U.S. 1993*, p. 88, Table 25; p. 89, Table 26; p. 220, Table 125. Figures for life expectancy are for 1989; for health spending per capita, 1990.

7.9 *Health, U.S. 1993*, p. 101, Table 63; p. 117, Table 78.

7.10 *SWA 1994-95*, p. 301, Figure 7C. Note: "Richest fifth" is a weighted average of the top 5% and the next 15%. "Family income" in this case includes money income, employer payments for health insurance, employer's share of payroll tax, and corporate income taxes.

7.11 DHHS, *Health, U.S. 1993*, p. 82, Table 20. *NHPB*, p. 64.

7.12 DHHS, *Health, U.S. 1993 Chartbook*, pp. 7, 49.

7.13 DHHS, *Health, U.S. 1993 Chartbook*, p. 49.

7.14 Robert J. Blendon, Robert Leitman, Ian Morrison, and Karen Donelan, "Satisfaction with Health Systems in Ten Nations," *Health Affairs* 9, no. 2 (Summer 1990), p. 188.

7.15 *Global Outlook 2000* (UN, 1990), p. 10, Table 1.1; pp. 302-03, Tables 12.2 and 12.3. *Report on the World Social Situation 1993* (UN, 1993), p. 37. Text: *Global Outlook*, pp. 285-300. B. H. Liese and P. S. Sachdeva, "Organizing Tropical Disease Control," *Finance and Development* (Dec. 1993), pp. 44-46. Greg Easterbrook, "Forget PCBs, Radon, Alar," *NYT Magazine*, 9/11/94, pp. 60-63.

7.16 Jonathan Mann, Daniel Tarantola, and Thomas Netter, eds., *AIDS in the World* (Cambridge: Harvard University Press, 1992), p. 478. Text: U.N., *Report on the World Social Situation 1993*, pp. 39-41.

Chapter 8: Environment

8.1 Herman E. Daly and John B. Cobb, Jr., *For the Common Good: Redirecting the Economy Toward Community, the Environment, and a Sustainable Future* (Boston: Beacon Press, 1994), p. 462-63, Table A-1.

8.2 Andrew Rees, *The Pocket Green Book: The Environ-

mental Crisis in a Nutshell (London: Zed Books, 1991), pp. 10-11. Emily Yoffe, "Silence of the Frogs," *NYT Magazine*, 12/13/92, p. 36.

8.3   Sandra Postel, "Carrying Capacity: Earth's Bottom Line," in Lester Brown, et al., eds., *State of the World, 1994* (New York: W. W. Norton, 1994), p. 10.

8.4   *SA 1994*, p. 237, Table 377. Note: "Endangered" is defined as in danger of becoming extinct throughout all or a significant part of its natural range. Text: "Listing of Endangered Species Said to Come Too Late to Help," *NYT*, 3/16/93, p. C-4.

8.5   *SA 1994*, p. 235, Table 372. Text: Michael Weisskopf, "EPA Plans to Cut Payments to Superfund Contractors," *WP*, 10/3/91, p. A-25. Thomas Lippman, "Facing a Nightmare of Poisoned Earth," *WP*, 10/2/91, p. A-1.

8.6   *SA 1993*, p. 227, Table 372. Text: "More Trash Recycles but Volume Still Grows," *WSJ*, 8/25/92, p. B-1.

8.7   *SA 1987*, p. 189, Table 329. *SA 1994*, p. 230, Table 361. Text: Brad Knickerbocker, "Refining the Clean Water Act May Not Be Easy for Clinton," *CSM*, 2/8/94, p. 3.

8.8   *SA 1993*, p. 225, Table 368. Text: "Study Ties Fouled Air to High Urban Death Rates," *NYT*, 12/9/93, p. B-15.

8.9   *SA 1994*, p. 592, Table 934.

8.10   Marc Breslow, "Gluttons for Energy," *DS* 184 (March 1993), pp. 6-9.

8.11   Joe Alper, "Protecting the Environment with the Power of the Market," *Science* 260, no. 25 (June 1993), p. 1884. Richard D. Morgenstern, "The Market-Based Approach at EPA," *EPA Journal* (May-June 1992), pp. 27-28.

8.12   Sam Walker, "Mopping Up the Mess After Desert Storm," *CSM*, 12/15/92, p. 15. *Congressional Quarterly Researcher*, 12/17/92, pp. 39-40. Joni Seager, *Earth Follies: Coming to Feminist Terms with the Global Environmental Crisis* (New York: Routledge, 1993), p. 21. Stephanie Pain, "The Two Faces of the Exxon Disaster," *New Scientist*, 5/22/93, pp. 11-13. "After Valdez," *The Economist*, 6/18/94, p. 20. Jay M. Gould, "Chernobyl, the Hidden Tragedy," *The Nation*, 3/15/93, pp. 331-34. Molly Moore, "The Second Disaster in Bhopal," *Business and Society Review* (Winter 1994), pp. 26-28. Bernard Gwertzman, "Fire in Reactor May Be Out...," *NYT*, 5/2/86, p. A-1.

8.13   *SA 1994*, p. 334, Table 509. Note: Values for 1994 are estimated. Text: Jeff Bailey and Timothy Noah, "EPA Spending Is Off Target, Study Says," *WSJ*, 5/24/94, p. B-1.

8.14   *SA 1993*, p. 229, Table 377. *SA 1994*, p. 236, Table 374.

8.15   D.R. Wernette and L.A. Nieves, "Breathing Polluted Air," *EPA Journal* 18, no. 1 (Mar.-Apr. 1992), pp. 16-17. Robert D. Bullard, "In Our Backyards," *EPA Journal* 18 (Mar.-Apr. 1992), p. 12. United Church of Christ Commission for Racial Justice, *Toxic Wastes and Race in the United States* (New York: United Church of Christ, 1987). Joni Seager, *Earth Follies: Coming to Feminist Terms with the Global Environmental Crisis* (New York: Routledge, 1993), pp. 158-60. See also Robert D. Bullard, *Dumping in Dixie: Race, Class and Environmental Quality* (Boulder, CO: Westview Press, 1990).

8.16   Michael Weisskopf, "World Bank Official's Irony Backfires," *WP*, 2/10/92, p. A-9. Paul Lewis, "Western Nations, Except for U.S., Ban Export of Hazardous Waste," *NYT*, 3/26/94, p. 3. Center for Investigative Reporting and Bill Moyers, *Global Dumping*

Ground: The International Traffic in Hazardous Waste (Arlington, VA: Seven Locks Press, 1990), pp. 6, 58-61.

Chapter 9: Macroeconomics

9.1 *ERP 1995* p. 268, Table B-1; p. 406, Table B-114; p. 278, Table B-3.

9.3 *ERP 1995* p. 274, Table B-1; p. 398, Table B-114; p. 278, Table B-3.

9.4 *ERP 1994*, p. 329, Table B-48. Note: 1994 figure based on average of first 3 quarters.

9.5 *ERP 1991*, p. 300, Table B-12; p. 304, Table B-16. *ERP 1995*, p. 290, Table B-13; p. 294, Table B-17. Text: Bradford DeLong and Larry Summers, "Equipment Investment and Economic Growth: How Strong Is the Nexus?" *Brookings Papers on Economic Activity* 2 (1992), pp. 157-99.

9.6 *ERP 1991*, p. 318, Table B-28. *ERP 1993*, p. 474, Table B-111. *ERP 1995*, p. 274, Table B-1; p. 308, Table B-29. Note: 1994 data based on average of first 3 quarters.

9.7 *ERP 1991*, p. 293, Table B-5. *ERP 1994*, p. 276, Table B-5; p. 352, Table B-72. *Moody's Bond Record* 61, no. 11 (Nov. 1994), p. 27. *SCB* 74, no. 9 (Sept. 1994), p. 21, Table 7.14. Note: Rates for 1994 are derived from numbers for the first 2 quarters of that year.

9.9 *SA 1987*, p. 524, Table 894. *SA 1993*, p. 543, Table 869. "1992 M&A Profile," *Mergers and Acquisitions* 27, no. 6 (May-June 1993), p. 46. "1993 M&A Profile," *Mergers and Acquisitions* 28, no. 6 (May-June 1994), p. 46.

9.10 *NIPA 1929-82*, pp. 61-62, Table 1.16. *NIPA 1959-88*, pp. 39-40, Table 1.16. *SCB* 64, no. 7, p. 31, Table 1.13. *SCB*, 70, no. 9, p. 6, Table 1.16. *SCB* 71, no. 9, p. 6, Table 1.16.

SCB 72, no. 9, p. 8, Table 1.16. *SCB* 73, no. 9, p. 10, Table 1.16. *SCB* 74, no. 9, p. 9, Table 1.16

9.11 *ERP 1995*, p. 386, Table B-97.

9.12 Resolution Trust Corporation, *RTC Review* (Jan. 1994), pp. 12-14. "Fortunate Sons," Briefing Paper, Southern Finance Project, Sept. 9, 1992. Robert Sherill, "S&Ls, Big Banks and Other Triumphs of Capitalism," *The Nation*, 11/19/90, pp. 589-623. Bradley R. Schiller, *The Economy Today* (New York: McGraw-Hill, 1994), p. 9.

9.13 Roger J. Vaughan and Edward W. Hill, *Banking on the Brink* (WP Co. Briefing Books, 1992), pp. 134-35.

9.14 *BS 1945-93*, pp. 20-25, Table B-100.

9.15 See *NIPA* and *SCB* citations for 9.10. *BS 1945-1993*, pp. 32-37, Table B-104. Note: "Capital stock" is defined as the value of nonresidential plant and equipment.

9.16 *ERP 1991*, p. 393, Table B-93. *ERP 1994*, p. 377, Table B-94. *Barron's*, 12/12/94, p. MW97. Note: 1994 based on average of first 3 quarters.

Chapter 10: The Global Economy

10.1 World Bank, *World Tables 1994* (Baltimore, MD: Johns Hopkins University Press, 1994), pp. 292-3, 372-73, 692-93. *World Tables 1991*, pp. 264-65, 340-41, 604-5.

10.2 "Managing Productivity," McKinsey Global Institute, Washington, DC, Oct. 1993, Exhibit S-1, p. 1.

10.3 *International Financial Statistics Yearbook 1992* (Washington: International Monetary Fund, 1992), pp. 366-67, 438-39, 720-21. *International Financial Statistics Yearbook 1993* (Washington: International Monetary Fund, 1993), pp. 368-69, 440-41, 726-27.

Text: Lawrence Summers and J. Bradford de Long, "Equipment Investment and Economic Growth: How Strong Is the Nexus?" *Brookings Papers on Economic Activity* 2 (1992), pp. 157-99. Michael Porter, "Capital Disadvantage: America's Failing Capital Investment System," *Harvard Business Review* 70, no. 5 (Sept.-Oct. 1992), pp. 65-82. Note: Before 1991, "Germany" refers exclusively to West Germany.

10.4 National Science Board, National Science Foundation, *Science Indicators* (Washington: GPO, 1985), p. 190. *SA 1990*, p. 585, Table 990. *SA 1993*, p. 598, Table 979. *SA 1994*, p. 610, Table 970. Note: Numbers to 1989 are percentage of GNP; numbers for 1990 are percentage of GDP. Text: *WSJ*, 11/16/88, p. A-1. *NYT*, 10/30/92, pp. C-1, C-9. "The Global Patent Race Picks Up Speed," *BW*, 8/9/93, p. 57.

10.5 *ERP 1995*, p. 278, Table B-3; pp. 395, Table B-105; p. 406, Table B-116.

10.6 Department of Commerce, *U.S. Industrial Outlook 1986* (Washington: GPO), pp. 28-1, 28-8. *U.S. Industrial Outlook 1994*, p. 26-1. Text: *Fortune*, 4/16/94, pp. 60-64.

10.8 BLS, *International Comparisons of Hourly Compensation Costs for Production Workers in Manufacturing, 1992*, Report 844 (April 1993), p. 6, Table 2.

10.9 *SA 1994*, p. 811, Table 1316.

10.10 *NIPA 1929-58*, p. 19, Tables 1.14 and 1.15. *NIPA 1959-88*, p. 29, Table 1.14; p. 37, Table 1.15. Text: UNCTAD, Programme on Transnational Corporations, *World Investment Report 1993* (New York: UN, 1993), pp. 26-27, Table 1.10. *SCB* (Feb. 1994), pp. 42-63.

10.11 UN, *Report on the World Social Situation* (1993), p. 81. Note: "Developed nations" are defined as members of OECD. Text: UN, *World Economic Survey* (1993), p. 209.

10.12 UN, *Global Outlook 2000* (1990), p. 10, Table 1.1.

10.13 United Nations Development Programme, *Human Development Report 1993* (New York: Oxford University Press, 1993), pp. 142-43. Text: World Bank, *Social Indicators of Development 1990* (Baltimore, MD: Johns Hopkins University Press, 1991), pp. 40-41, 70-71, 270-71, 288-89.

10.14 World Food Council, *The Global State of Hunger and Malnutrition* (New York, 1992) p. 8, Table 2. Text: UN, *Report on the World Social Situation* (1993), pp. 28-33.

10.15 *The Economist Book of Vital World Statistics* (New York: Times Books and Random House, 1990), pp. 86-102. World Bank, *World Tables 1994* (Baltimore, MD: Johns Hopkins University Press, 1992), pp. 202-03, 254-55, 298-99, 314-15, 330-31, 430-31, 478-79, 522-23.

10.16 *WDR 1994*, pp. 206-07, Tables 23 and 24.

Glossary

Affirmative action. A plan or program to remedy the effects of past racial or sexual discrimination in employment and to prevent its recurrence. Unlike antidiscrimination or equal opportunity laws, which forbid unequal treatment, affirmative action requires positive corrective measures. Affirmative action usually involves the establishment of goals and timetables to increase use of underrepresented classes of persons.

Aid to Families with Dependent Children (AFDC). Financial aid provided under the assistance program of the Social Security Act of 1935 for children who lack adequate support but are living with one parent or relative. The program is administered by the states with the assistance of federal funds under regulations established by the federal government.

Antitrust law. Legislation designed to control the growth of market power exercised by firms. "Market power" refers to monopoly and restraint of trade by individual firms, groups of amalgamated companies (trusts), and groups of cooperating firms (cartels).

Asset. Anything of value that is owned. See *Financial assets.*

Baby boom. The period of high birthrates in the U.S. following World War II through 1964.

Balance of payments. The difference between the total payments into and out of a country during a period of time. It includes such items as all merchandise trade, tourist expenditures, capital movements, and interest charges.

Bond. An IOU or promissory note from a corporation or government. A bond is evidence of a debt on which the issuer (borrower) usually promises to pay a specified amount of interest for a specified period of time and usually to repay the principal on the date of expiration, or maturity date. A bond represents debt whose main purpose is to raise capital. There are many types of bonds: those issued by a central government (government bond, Treasury bond), a local government (municipal bond), or a corporation (corporate bond).

Bureau of Labor Statistics. The principal fact-finding agency on labor economics issues, a division of the Department of Labor.

Business cycle. The pattern of medium-term economic fluctuations in which expansion is followed by recession, which is followed by expansion, and so on.

Capital gain. The difference between the purchase price of an asset and its resale price at some later date. It is called a "capital loss" if the resale price is less than the purchase price.

Capital goods. Machinery, equipment, and structures used in the production of goods and services.

Capitalist. One who owns capital goods used in production and exercises control over the labor of others. He or she receives income in the form of profits.

Capital stock. The sum of capital goods in an economy.

Child support payments. Payments made by one parent of a child to the other parent for the express purpose of maintaining that child's welfare. Sometimes a divorce settlement will be comprised of both alimony (payments to support an ex-spouse) and child support payments.

Commercial banks. Privately owned banks that receive deposits and make loans. Commercial banks issue time and savings deposits, operate trust departments, act as agents in buying and selling securities, and underwrite and sell new security issues for state and local governments. All U.S. national banks and some state banks are commercial banks.

Concentration. The extent to which an industry is dominated by a small number of firms. The concentration ratio measures the percentage of total assets, production, employment, sales, or profits accounted for by top firms.

Conglomerate. A corporation which competes in multiple, not necessarily related industries. A conglomerate often acquires its large, diversified holdings through mergers and/or acquisitions.

Comparable worth. A method for establishing a wage and salary structure across occupations whereby an occupation's wage rate or salary is based on certain characteristics, such as responsibility and working conditions, in comparison with other occupations. Also called *pay equity*.

Consumer Price Index (CPI). A measure of the average change in prices over time in a fixed "market basket" of goods and services purchased either by urban wage earners and clerical workers (CPI-W) or by all urban consumers (CPI-U).

Corporate income tax. A tax imposed on the annual net earnings of a corporation. In the U.S., such taxes are levied by the federal government and by most states on all incorporated business. The corporate income tax rate depends on the size of earnings.

Corporation. A form of business organization consisting of an association of owners, called "stockholders," who are regarded as a single entity (person) in the eyes of the law. The chief advantages of the corporation are limited liability (each stockholder is liable for the debts of the business only to the extent of his investment), simple transfer of ownership (anyone can buy or sell stock at any time), and continuity, or permanence (the corporation continues to exist even if all the owners die). Created by statute law which varies from state to state, a corporation has no legal status outside of the state in which it is chartered.

Cost-of-living allowance (COLA). An increase in wages, based on a Consumer Price Index, intended to keep them in line with the current cost of living.

Cost of production. The total cost of materials, labor, and overhead charges (such as rent and electricity) incurred in production.

Demand. The quantity of a commodity which a consumer or consumers as a whole would be willing and able to purchase.

Department of Energy (DOE). Established in 1977, this Cabinet-level department exercises primary responsibility for policies, programs, and administration in the energy field. It also manages the nuclear weapons program.

Depreciation. The cost, due to wear and tear, aging, and/or technological obsolescence, of restoring the capital goods used in producing last year's output.

Depression. A prolonged period in which business activity is at a very low level. Production is greatly reduced, there is little or no new capital investment, income is sharply lowered, there is massive unemployment, many businesses fail, and banks are slow to create credit.

Deregulation. The lessening of government control over the operations of various industries, a policy that began to be applied in the United States in the late 1970s to the transportation industries (airlines, air freight, trucking, railroads) and to financial institutions (commercial banks, thrift institutions, brokerage houses).

Direct foreign investment. Establishment or purchase of a controlling interest in a foreign business or subsidiary, which usually involves managerial control over the business.

Discount rate. The interest rate charged by Federal Reserve banks on loans to their member banks. Discount rates are set every 14 days by the regional Federal Reserve banks, subject to approval by the Board of Governors.

Discouraged workers. Workers who have become so disheartened by their fruitless search for employment that they give up the attempt and withdraw from the labor force. The official unemployment rate is understated to the extent that discouraged workers are not counted in unemployment measures.

Dividends. A payment to shareholders in a company, in the form of cash or shares, in proportion to their share of ownership.

Division of labor. Specialization of productive activity either by persons in different occupational groups undertaking particular tasks or by dividing a task into its component operations.

Dow Jones Industrial Average. An average of stock prices that serves as a barometer of the market as a whole. This average, calculated daily, is based on 30 industrial stocks.

Durable good. A good which can be used repeatedly or over a number of periods.

Economic expansion. That part or phase of the business cycle when total output and employment rise.

Employee stock ownership plan (ESOP). Also called "employee stock purchase plan," an ESOP permits employees to purchase stock in the company which employs them, often at discount from the current market price, by means of payroll deductions. While giving employees partial ownership of the firms assets, ESOPs usually confer little or no control over the assets. ESOPs also are a cheap way for a firm to raise financial capital.

Environmental Protection Agency (EPA). An independent federal agency created in 1970 which deals with pollution in the areas of air, water, solid waste, noise, radiation, and toxic substances.

Equal Employment Opportunity Commission (EEOC) An independent federal agency established by the Civil Rights Act of 1964 to help end racial and sexual discrimination in employment practices and promote voluntary affirmative action. The EEOC stresses confidential persuasion and conciliation to achieve its objectives. Though given authority in 1972 to institute legal actions if conciliation fails, the EEOC lacks authority to issue cease and desist orders.

Equal Pay Act. The 1963 labor law which prohibits discrimination in pay on the basis of race or gender.

Export. Any good or service sold to a foreign country.

Externality. The effect of one economic activity on

another person, firm, or sector not part of (external to) that activity. The effect may be beneficial or harmful.

Federal budget deficit. A deficit occurs when government expenditures exceed income (tax receipts).

Federal Reserve Bank. The central bank of the United States. Its main purpose is to maintain and enhance the viability and stability of the monetary system. The "Fed" operates under a system of 12 Federal Reserve banks owned by the member banks in their respective districts.

Financial assets. Assets that are financial in character, such as cash, stocks, bonds, or government securities.

Firm. A business entity under one ownership. Proprietorships (owned by one person), partnerships (owned by two or more people), and corporations are all firms.

Fiscal policy. The policy of using government spending and taxation to affect some aspect of the economy, especially levels of unemployment and inflation.

Food stamps. A welfare program to improve nutrition in low-income households. The food stamp program is administered by the Department of Agriculture through state and local welfare agencies, which establish eligibility, issue stamps, and maintain controls.

Government transfers (transfer payments). Payments which are not made in return for some productive service; for example, payments made by the state to needy individuals which, in effect, transfer income from wealthier sectors of the population to the poorer.

Gross domestic product (GDP). A measure of the total value of goods and services produced within the country over a specified time period, normally a year. Income arising from investments abroad is not included.

Gross national product (GNP). A measure of the value of the goods and services produced by the residents of the country (regardless of where the assets are located) over a specified time period, normally a year. It includes income from U.S. investments abroad.

Householder. The person (or one of the persons) in whose name the housing unit is owned or rented. The U.S. Census describes other members of the household in terms of their relationship to the householder.

Import. Any good or service purchased from a foreign country.

Infant mortality rate. The number of infants per 1,000 born that die within the first year of life.

Inflation. A general increase in prices, often measured by an increase in the Consumer Price Index.

Infrastructure. Basic facilities and services upon which an economy's industry and commerce depend. Included are transportation systems, sanitation, communications networks, and public utilities.

International Monetary Fund. An institution affiliated with the United Nations, set up at the Bretton Woods Conference in 1944 to promote international monetary cooperation, facilitate the growth of international trade, and make the fund's resources available to members.

Investment (capital). A purchase of capital goods that will be used directly in production of goods and services.

Investment (financial). The purchase of any financial asset, such as a stock or bond. Distinguished from the purchase of productive capital, such as plant or equipment.

Labor intensive. Utilizing a large proportion of labor input relative to capital investment.

Labor force. Those persons who have jobs or are actively looking for jobs.

Labor force participation rate. The proportion of the working-age population that is part of the labor force.

Leading indicator. An statistic that anticipates the ups and downs of the business cycle. Among those indicators considered most important are the average workweek of manufacturing production workers, average weekly initial claims for state unemployment insurance, the money supply, and new orders for consumer and capital goods.

Liabilities. The claims of creditor. The assets of an individual or business are subject to payment of these claims.

Macroeconomics. The study of the behavior of the economy as a whole, focusing on variables such as employment, inflation, growth, and stability.

Mean. See *Toolkit*, section T.3.

Median. See *Toolkit*, section T.3.

Medicaid. Some poor persons who need medical services but do not qualify for Medicare are assisted under this federally supported state system, established in 1960.

Medicare. A health insurance program enacted in 1965 as an amendment to the Social Security Act to provide medical care for the elderly. Two health care programs are involved. One is compulsory and financed by increases in the Social Security payroll tax, covering most hospital and nursing home costs for persons age 65 or older. The second is a voluntary supplemental health program for persons over 65, which covers a variety of health services both in and out of medical institutions and pays a substantial part of physician costs. The supplemental plan is financed by a small charge to the person enrolled and by an equal amount paid by the federal government out of general revenue.

Merger. The fusion of two or more separate companies into one. In current usage, a merger is a special case in which both the merging companies wish to join together and do so on roughly equal terms.

Microeconomics. The study of individual decision-making in response to changes in prices and incomes.

Minimum wage. The lowest wage, established by federal law, which can be paid by an employer. Some states also have minimum wages.

Monetary policy. The use of monetary controls such as restriction or expansion of the money supply and manipulation of interest rates in order to achieve some desired policy objective, such as the control of inflation, an improvement in the balance of payments, a certain level of employment, or growth in the GNP.

Monopoly. Strictly speaking, a monopoly exists when a firm or individual produces and sells the entire output of some commodity. The lack of competition confers market power on the monopoly firm.

Mortgage. A legal agreement that creates an interest in real estate or transfers title to personal property as security for the payment of a debt. It is often viewed as a claim against or right in property.

Multinational corporation. A company that has operation centers in many countries, as opposed to an international company, which imports or exports goods but has its operation centered in one country.

Mutual fund. An open-end investment trust which gives its management discretion in the choice of investment.

Net domestic product. GDP minus depreciation.

Net national product. GNP minus depreciation.

Net worth. The total assets of a person or business less the total liabilities (amounts due to creditors).

Nondurable goods. Goods which are used up very rapidly or after a single use.

Nonfinancial corporate assets. Physical assets (such as plant, equipment, and inventories) and other assets (such as accounts receivable).

Organization for Economic Cooperation and Development (OECD). A 24-member international, intergovernmental agency founded in 1961 to promote policies leading to optimum economic growth, employment, and living standard in member countries while maintaining financial stability. The OECD reviews economic problems of members, conducts research, collects and disseminates statistics on its member countries, and issues publications. It includes 19 European nations, Canada, the U. S., Japan, Australia, and New Zealand.

Organization of Petroleum Exporting Countries (OPEC). An international organization which seeks to coordinate petroleum production and pricing policies in member petroleum exporting countries. The organization was formally established in 1960. Its activities have evolved from maintaining export price floors and coordinating production programs to negotiating petroleum export price and production ceilings and providing financial assistance for developing countries. Member nations include Iran, Iraq, Kuwait, Libya, Saudi Arabia, Venezuela, Algeria, Ecuador, Gabon, Indonesia, Nigeria, Qatar, and the United Arab Emirates.

Overhead. A general term for all business costs that are neither direct labor (the wage paid to production workers) nor direct material (the stuff the product is made of). Examples of overhead are indirect labor costs (such as wages and salaries paid to inspectors, material handlers, and supervisors) and fringe benefits paid to all employees.

Pay equity. See *Comparable worth.*

Pension fund. Sums of money laid aside and normally invested to provide a regular income in retirement or in compensation for disablement.

Per Capita. A Latin term meaning "for each person."

Political action committee (PAC). A group of people, usually professionals, that lobbies Congress. PACs raise substantial amounts of money for candidates of their choice.

Poverty line. See *Toolkit,* section T.10.

Poverty rate. The percentage of the population with incomes under the poverty line. See *Toolkit,* section T.10.

Present value. The present value of a sum of money expected in the future is the amount one would need to invest at current interest rates to obtain that future sum of money by the specified date. The present value of a past sum of money is what it would be worth today had it been invested at then-current interest rates.

Private sector. All economic activities that are independent of government control (or outside the so-called *public sector*), carried on principally for profit but also including nonprofit organizations directed at satisfying private needs, such as private hospitals and private schools. Included are enterprises owned individually or by groups, and the self-employed.

Productive capacity. The potential output of a business with existing plant, workers, and equipment.

Productivity. The efficiency with which productive resources are used. Most commonly applied to labor.

Profit rate. The ratio of a company's profits to the value of its capital stock.

Progressive tax structure. A tax structure in which the tax rate rises with income. Most income tax systems in Western countries are progressive.

Protectionism. The policy of imposing import restrictions, such as tariffs (taxes) or quotas (quantity limits) on imported goods in order to protect domestic industries.

Public sector. That part of the economy which is publicly rather than privately owned. It includes all government departments and agencies and all public corporations such as electricity and water boards.

Real earnings. Earnings after the effects of inflation have been taken into account.

Real interest rate. The interest rate minus the anticipated rate of inflation; what a borrower is actually paying for the use of money.

Recession. That part or phase of the business cycle in which total output falls; during recession, investment usually declines, and the demand for labor is reduced, so unemployment rises.

Regressive tax. A tax that takes a larger proportion of low incomes than of high.

Renewable sources of energy. Energy sources that are not depleted by use, such as solar power.

Revenue neutral. A revenue-neutral tax bill is one that does not affect overall tax revenues.

Savings. All income not spent on goods and services used for current consumption. Both firms and households save.

Social Security. Officially known as "Old Age, Survivors, and Disability Insurance" ("OASDI"), its major purposes are to provide retirement income for thr elderly, income for workers who are totally disabled, income for spouses and children of deceased wage earners, and Medicare. All eligible workers are required to contribute a certain percentage of their income, to be matched by their employer. These contributions are credited to each worker's account; upon death, retirement, or disablement, funds are allocated in accordance with the formulas provided by law.

Social spending. Spending by government agencies to increase the welfare of individuals and the community as a whole. As used in this book, the term does not include expenditures on Social Security or Medicare.

Spendable earnings. Earnings after all taxes have been deducted.

Standard of living. The level of material well-being of an individual or household.

Stocks. Certificates or claims of ownership interests in a corporation. Stocks entitle the owner to dividend payments from the corporation.

Tax loophole. A legal provision that can be used to reduce one's tax liability. Such provisions may be unintentional discrepancies in the law, or they may be intended to benefit an industry or group.

Terms of trade. The purchasing power of a country's exports in terms of the imports that they will buy.

Trade deficit. The amount by which a nation's imports exceed its exports of merchandise over a given period.

Unemployment. The nonavailability of jobs for persons able and willing to work at the prevailing wage rate. It is an important measure of the performance of an economy. Full employment is generally considered a highly desirable goal.

Unemployment insurance. A program of insurance established by the Social Security Act of 1935 that provides for the payment of funds for a limited period of time to workers who are laid off or discharged for reasons beyond their control. Under the plan, Congress imposes a tax on the payroll of employers of 4 or more workers. Proceeds of the tax are held by the Treasury Department in separate state accounts. Each state determines the amount, duration, and conditions of payments to unemployed persons.

Union. An organization of workers formed for the purpose of collective bargaining with employers concerning wages, working hours, job security, fringe benefits, seniority, and similar matters of common interest.

Worker participation. A form of workplace democracy where workers directly exercise power over the firm's decisions.

World Bank. An institution affiliated with the United Nations and set up at the Bretton Woods Conference in 1944, whose chief purposes is to assist in the reconstruction and development of its poor members by facilitating capital investment, making loans, and promoting foreign investment.